Colorful, Casual, & Comfy Quilts

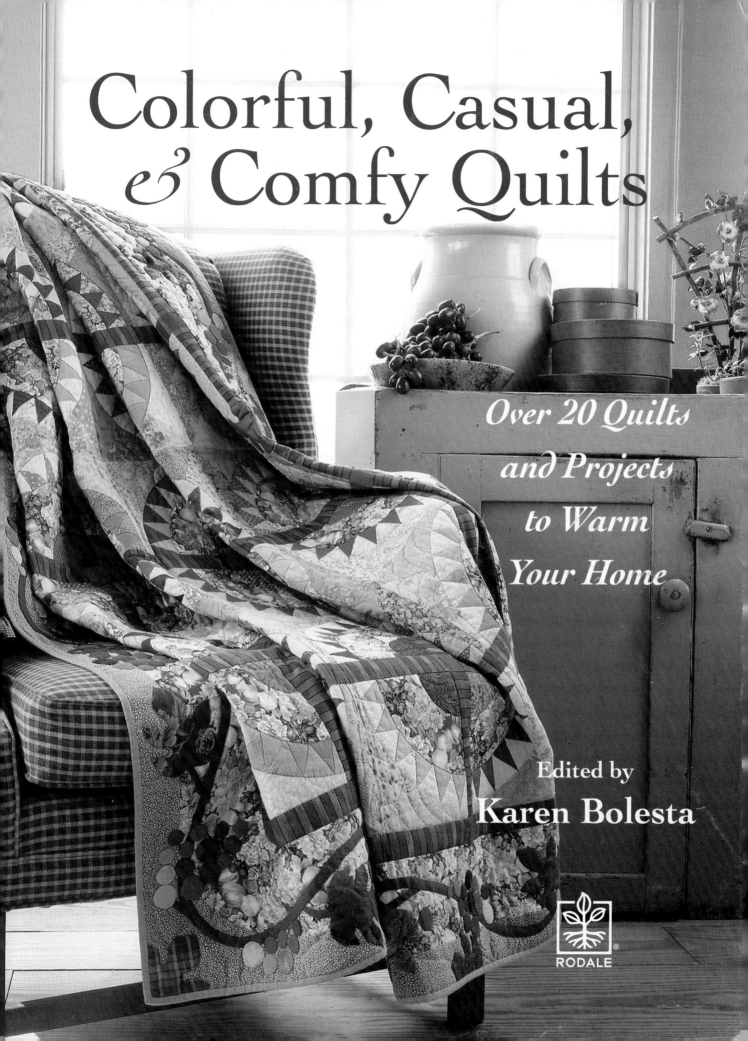

Colorful, Casual, & Comfy Quilts

Over 20 Quilts and Projects to Warm Your Home

Edited by
Karen Bolesta

RODALE

Editor: Karen Bolesta

Photographer: Mitch Mandel

Project Illustrator: Sandy Freeman

Tips & Techniques Illustrator: Charles Metz

Additional Illustration by: Ann Nunemacher (Princess Feather and Rose of Sharon)

Library of Congress Cataloging-in-Publication Data

Colorful, casual & comfy quilts : over 20 quilts and projects
 to warm your home / edited by Karen Bolesta
    p. cm
    ISBN 1–57954–845–9 paperback
1. Patchwork—patterns. 2. Quilting—Patterns. 3. Patchwork quilts. Bolesta, Karen.
TT835.C6475 2003
746.46'041—dc21   2003046695

Distributed to the book trade by St. Martin's Press

2 4 6 8 10 9 7 5 3 1   paperback

WE **INSPIRE** AND **ENABLE** PEOPLE TO IMPROVE
THEIR LIVES AND THE WORLD AROUND THEM

FOR MORE OF our PRODUCTS

WWW.RODALESTORE.COM
(800) 848-4735

Contents

Introduction

Every night I sleep under a quilt my maternal grandmother made. It's not an award-winner by any means; the hand-pieced 1940s Double Wedding Ring features patches cut from my "Mom-Mom's" old dresses, kitchen aprons, children's clothing, and dime-store piece goods. Mom-Mom passed away when I was in fourth grade so I have only a few memories of her, and to my dismay, I have absolutely no memories of her doing handwork.

A few years back, I decided to take her quilt tops and unassembled blocks out of the trunk in my guest room and finish them into quilts. You may think I had a treasure trove awaiting me, but I

Like many quilters of her generation, she only pieced traditional patterns and it was obvious that she learned as she went along.

wasn't enthralled with what was packed away. I'd seen many quilts like my grandmother's quilts—made with lots of love but a little shy in the beauty and perfection departments. My grandmother's quilt tops and blocks were mismatched patches of colors and calicoes with a good measure of Depression green and bubblegum pink fabrics thrown in, too. Like many quilters of her generation, she

only pieced traditional patterns—Grandmother's Flower Garden, Trip Around the World, and Double Wedding Ring—and it was obvious that she learned as she went along. To be honest, these quilts weren't the kind of quilts you unfolded for Sunday guests to admire; these were rag bag scrap quilts intended to keep a family warm at night, plain and simple.

I only had one goal in mind when I unpacked the antique wooden trunk that day—get the four or five quilt tops in a suitable condition and have a charitable group hand-quilt them. I had so many of my own unfinished quilts in my sewing room that I knew I'd never take the time to finish and hand-quilt my grandmother's quilt tops, too.

The Double Wedding Ring quilt was in the best shape so that's what I tackled first. The quilt featured an unusual mix of pink and orangey calicoes. The fabrics were so busy and patterned that it was hard to tell where the background ended and the wedding rings began. Add in the bright pink border and it was surely a sight only the quilt-maker could love. I cut hundreds of threads off the back of the quilt, repaired a number of weak seams, pressed it, added a wide border of repro-

I threw the quilt unceremoniously on my bed and was nearly bowled over by its beauty.

duction fabric, pieced a muslin backing, and shipped the quilt top, batting, and backing off to a group of quilters who met at a local library.

A few months later I got the call that the quilt was done. I threw the quilt unceremoniously on my bed and was nearly bowled over by its beauty. It didn't matter that the fabrics competed with one another or that the pink border shouted out loud, I simply fell in love with the quilt. The thousands and thousands of tiny quilting stitches those six ladies made turned that ugly duckling of a quilt into a beautiful swan. The quilt was gently rippled from the stitches, making it look as if it had been

It's colorful, casual, and comfy, and I love it that way.

keeping someone warm for decades. The quilting stitches brought the wedding ring arcs to life and turned those long pink borders into a landscape of dimpled valleys just begging you to run your hand over them.

It was the beginning of a love affair with my grandmother's quilts. The quilters at the library have quilted two more of her quilt tops for me, and they just put the third one in their quilting frame. This third quilt is a Grandmother's Flower Garden featuring more of Mom-Mom's favorite bubblegum

pink fabric—a bit loud for my taste, but obviously just perfect for hers. I'm sure the nimble fingers of the quiltie ladies will work magic once again.

Since the day I opened that trunk, I've learned a lot about family legacies. Sure, show-stopping quilts are nice to dream about and even make (and a real treasure if you find one among your grandmother's linens), but often it's the unassuming hand-me-downs or traditional quilt designs that take your breath away. I surely wouldn't trade my heirloom for anything! It's colorful, casual, and comfy, and I love it that way.

As you page through this book, you'll see one memorable quilt after another—some perfectly pieced and others of a more casual nature. That's one of the reasons why I love quilting so much. No matter what our skill level, we each bring our experiences, tastes, passions, and heart with us to the sewing machine. Beauty is certainly in the eye of the beholder (whether she's the original quiltmaker or a granddaughter using the quilt half a century later). Once a quilt is tossed on a bed and snuggled under each night, you can easily overlook a puckered or mismatched seam or two and see the love that is present in every quilting stitch.

Here's to heartwarming quilts!

Karen Bolesta

Prints Aplenty

■

Konnichiwa

Quiltmaker: Suzanne Marshall

*K*onnichiwa is a Japanese greeting meaning "Good afternoon." Suzanne's collection of blue and white oriental batik-style prints form the basis for this clean, graphic quilt design. The use of cool gray as the background neutral provides an unexpected—and elegant—touch.

Skill Level: Intermediate

Size: Finished quilt is 85½ × 98 inches
Finished block is 12 inches square

Fabrics and Supplies

NOTE: The yardages listed are for cutting each of the border and vertical sashing strips in the quilt as a single length of fabric.

- ✓ 2⅞ yards of dark red print fabric for the sashing strips, borders, and binding
- ✓ 2⅞ yards of light gray print fabric for the blocks and borders
- ✓ 2⅞ yards of medium gray print fabric for the blocks and borders
- ✓ 2 yards of white-on-white print fabric for the blocks
- ✓ 1¼ yards of navy blue print fabric for the blocks
- ✓ Scraps of 42 assorted dark red print fabrics for the blocks. An 8 × 8-inch piece of each is sufficient.
- ✓ Scraps of 20 assorted medium gray print fabrics for the blocks. A 14 × 18-inch piece of each is sufficient.
- ✓ Scraps of six assorted light gray print fabrics for the blocks. A 14 × 18-inch piece of each is sufficient.
- ✓ Scraps of assorted indigo and white or navy and white batik print fabrics. There are 42 blocks in this quilt. Each block requires a 4¾-inch cut center square. You may use all different fabrics or duplicate as desired.
- ✓ 7½ yards of fabric for the quilt back
- ✓ Queen-size quilt batting (90 × 108 inches)
- ✓ Rotary cutter, ruler, and mat
- ✓ Template material

Cutting

All measurements include ¼-inch seam allowances. Measurements for the borders are longer than needed; trim them to the necessary length when they are added to the quilt top. With the exception of pattern pieces A and B, instructions given are for quick cutting using a rotary cutter and ruler. In most cases, strips for rotary cutting are cut slightly longer than needed to allow for adjustment or error in cutting.

Make templates for A and B using the full-size pattern pieces on page 7. Cut pieces in the order listed.

From the 2⅞ yards of dark red print fabric, cut:
- Two 1½ × 102-inch strips for borders
- Two 1½ × 90-inch strips for borders
- Four 2½-inch strips lengthwise for the binding
- Five 1 × 90-inch strips for sashings
- Two 1 × 90-inch strips for borders
- Two 1 × 102-inch strips for borders
- Five 1 × 102-inch strips for sashing. Cut these strips into 1 × 12½-inch segments. You'll need a total of 36 segments.

From the 2⅞ yards of light gray print fabric, cut:
- Two 1¼ × 102-inch border strips
- Two 1¼ × 90-inch border strips
- One 2⅝ × 66-inch strip. Cut this strip into 2⅝-inch squares to make a total of 24 D squares.

From the 2⅞ yards of medium gray print fabric, cut:
- Two 1¾ × 102-inch border strips
- Two 1¾ × 90-inch border strips
- One 3½ × 30-inch strip. Cut this strip into eight 3½-inch squares to make a total of 8 F squares.
- One 4¼ × 18-inch strip. Cut this strip into four 4¼-inch squares; cut these squares in half diagonally in both directions to make 16 E triangles.

From the 2 yards of white-on-white print fabric, cut:
- 336 B triangles, using template B

From the 1¼ yards of navy blue print fabric, cut:
- Ten 4¼ × 44-inch strips. Cut these strips into eighty-four 4¼-inch squares; cut these squares in half diagonally in both directions to make 336 E triangles.

From the assorted dark red print scraps, cut:
• 336 A triangles in groups of 8, using template A

From each of the assorted medium gray scraps, cut:
• Two 3½ × 18-inch strips. Cut these strips into 3½-inch F squares. You'll need a total of 8 F squares from *each* fabric.
• One 4¼ × 18-inch strip. Cut this strip into four 4¼-inch squares; cut these squares in half diagonally in both directions to make 16 E triangles from *each* fabric.

From each of the assorted light gray print scraps, cut:
• Five 2⅝ × 14-inch strips. Cut these strips into 2⅝-inch D squares. You'll need a total of 24 D squares from *each* fabric.

From the assorted indigo and white or navy and white print scraps, cut:
• Forty-two 4¾-inch C squares

Piecing the Blocks

1. Referring to the **Block Diagram,** lay out the following pieces for one block: eight matching red A triangles, eight white B triangles, one indigo and white C square, four matching light gray D squares, eight navy E triangles, four matching medium gray E triangles, and four matching medium gray F squares.

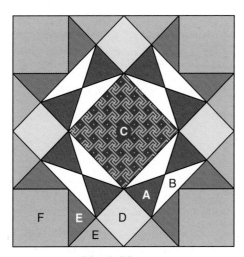

Block Diagram

2. Sew a red A triangle to a white B triangle, as shown in **Diagram 1**. Make eight of these units. Press the seam allowances toward the A pieces.

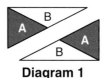

Diagram 1

3. Sew together two A/B units, as shown in **Diagram 2**. Make four of these units, pressing the seam allowance to one side.

Diagram 2

4. Sew a D square to each side of one of the A/B units, as shown in **Diagram 3**. Make two of these rows and press the seam allowances away from the D squares.

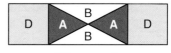

Diagram 3

5. Sew the remaining A/B units to each side of a C square as shown in **Diagram 4**. Press the seam allowance away from the C square, grading the seam allowance if necessary. For instructions on grading seam allowances, see page 155.

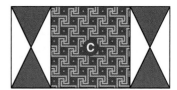

Diagram 4

6. Sew the rows together, as shown in **Diagram 5,** pinning carefully to match the seams. Press the seam allowances toward the center of the block.

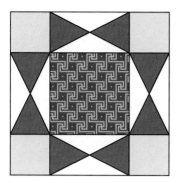

Diagram 5

7. Sew a navy E triangle to either side of an F square as shown in **Diagram 6.** Make four of these E/F units, pressing the seam allowances away from the F square.

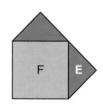

Diagram 6

8. Attach a gray E triangle to either side of each of the E/F units, as shown in **Diagram 7.** Press the seam allowances toward the gray E triangles.

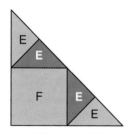

Diagram 7

9. Referring to the **Block Diagram,** sew one of the E/F triangle units to each side of the center block, pinning carefully to match the seams. Press the seam allowances toward the E/F triangle units. Make a total of 42 blocks.

Assembling the Quilt Top

1. Referring to the **Quilt Diagram** on page 6, lay out the blocks in six vertical rows of seven

blocks each. Insert a 1 × 12½-inch sashing strip between each block in each row. Sew the blocks and sashes together to complete the rows, trimming the seam allowances as necessary and pressing them away from the blocks.

2. Measure each of the completed vertical rows and take an average measurement. Trim the 1 × 89-inch sashing strips to this average measurement. Referring to the **Quilt Diagram,** insert a trimmed sashing strip between each of the vertical rows. Sew the rows and sashing strips together, taking care to align blocks horizontally before pinning and stitching. Ease as necessary for a proper fit. Trim the seam allowances as needed and press them away from the blocks.

Assembling and Adding the Borders

1. Referring to the **Border Diagram,** sew together along the long edge of the fabric, in order: a 1 × 90-inch dark red border strip, a 1¼ × 90-inch light gray border strip, a 1¾ × 90-inch medium gray border strip, a 1½ × 90-inch dark red border strip, a 1¾ × 90-inch medium gray border strip, and a 1¼ × 90-inch light gray border strip. Press all the seam allowances toward the dark red center strip. Make two of these border units, label them "top and bottom" and set them aside.

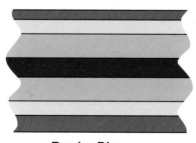

Border Diagram

2. Make two border units with the remaining 102-inch-long red and gray border strips, sewing them together in the order listed in Step 1. Label these units "left and right" and set them aside.

3. Sew the borders to the appropriate sides of the quilt, mitering each corner. For instructions on mitering, see page 160.

Quilt Diagram

Quilting and Finishing

1. Each block in this quilt is quilted in a simple pattern of carefully placed straight lines, and the borders are quilted in a combination of straight lines and a cable design, as shown in the **Border Quilting Diagram** and the **Block Quilting Diagram.**

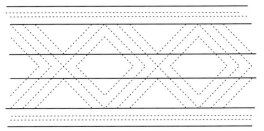

Border Quilting Diagram

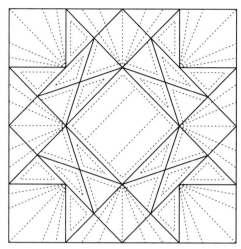

Block Quilting Diagram

3. Layer the quilt back, batting and quilt top. The backing fabric should extend beyond the quilt top equally, so that the center panel is centered. Baste the layers together and trim the quilt back and batting so that they are approximately 3 inches larger than the quilt top on all sides.

4. Quilt all marked designs and add additional quilting as desired. The quilt shown is quilted in navy blue quilting thread.

5. From the binding fabric, make approximately 380 inches of double-fold, straight-grain binding. The binding on the quilt shown finishes ½ inch wide, balancing the narrow red sashing and borders strips that are cut from the same fabric. To achieve this effect, cut binding strips 2½ inches wide. See page 164 for details on making and attaching binding.

6. Sew the binding to the quilt top. Trim the excess backing and batting, and use matching thread and an invisible stitch to hand-sew the folded edge of the binding to the back of the quilt.

2. Divide the backing fabric into three equal 90-inch-long pieces. Remove the selvages and sew the pieces together along the long edges. The seams will run parallel to the top and bottom of the quilt. Press the seams open.

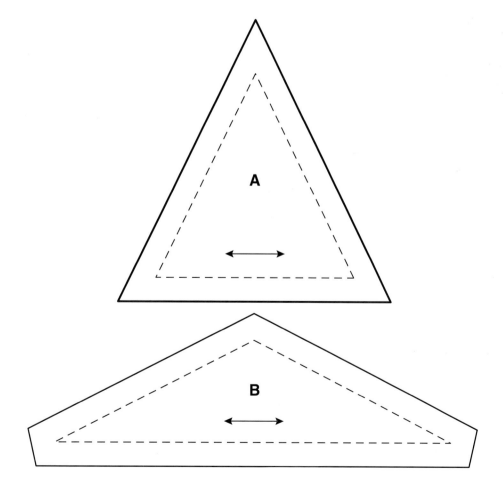

Overwhelmed by Autumn

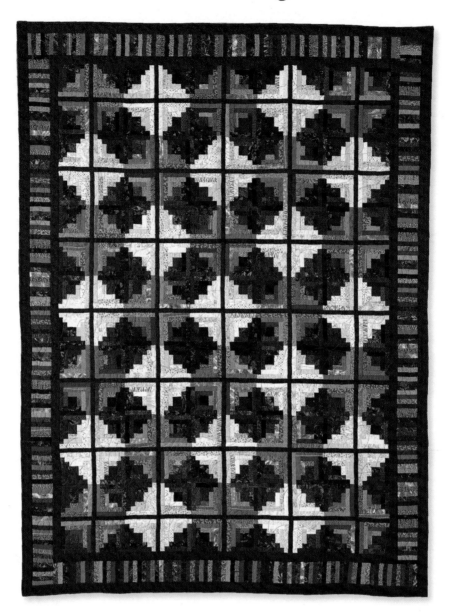

Quiltmaker: Diane Doro

Rich reds, browns, rusts, golds, and greens capture the essence of autumn as Diane saw it one lovely fall day as she and her husband were driving. Her new eyeglasses were bothering her too much to read, so she simply took them off and gazed out the window. Diane decided the fall colors were so beautiful when blurred together by her uncorrected vision that she just had to work them into a quilt!

Skill Level: Easy

Size: Finished quilt is approximately 69¾ × 92¼ inches
Finished Log Cabin unit is 5¼ inches square
Finished block is 10½ inches square

Fabrics and Supplies

- ✓ ¼ yard *each* of 14 assorted dark-value print fabrics, or scraps, to total 3½ yards for blocks and borders
- ✓ 3¼ yards of black with brown pindots fabric for borders, sashing, and binding
- ✓ ¼ yard *each* of 11 assorted medium-value print fabrics, or scraps, to total 2¾ yards for blocks and borders
- ✓ ¼ yard *each* of 7 assorted light-value print fabrics, or scraps, to total 1¾ yards for blocks
- ✓ 5½ yards of fabric for quilt back
- ✓ Full-size quilt batting (81 × 96 inches)
- ✓ Rotary cutter, ruler, and mat

Cutting

All measurements include ¼-inch seam allowances. The measurements for the borders include several extra inches in length; trim them to the exact length before sewing them to the quilt top. Instructions are given for quick-cutting all of the pieces using a rotary cutter and a ruler. Cut all strips across the fabric width unless directed otherwise. Note that for some of the pieces the quick-cutting method will result in left-over fabric.

You may want to cut just enough pieces to make one block to test your cutting and seam allowances for accuracy. If your finished block does not measure the size stated above, you can make adjustments before cutting all your fabric.

From the assorted dark fabrics, cut:
- 140 A squares: Cut one 2-inch strip from *each* of seven different fabrics (seven strips total).

From these strips, cut 140 squares, each 2 inches square.
- 140 *each* of pieces D, E, H, and I: Cut fifty-five 1¼-inch strips. Refer to "Cutting Chart for Log Cabin Pieces" for lengths to cut the pieces from the strips.
- Twenty-four 1¼-inch strips for border strip sets

From the black with brown pindots fabric, cut a 99-inch-long piece. From this piece, cut:
- Eight 2 × 99-inch borders cut *lengthwise*
- Seven 1¼ × 58-inch sashing strips cut *lengthwise*
- Thirty 1¼-inch strips cut *crosswise*. From these strips cut:

   Thirty 11-inch sashing strips
   Ten 5¾-inch sashing strips
- Reserve the remaining fabric for binding

From the assorted medium fabrics, cut:
- 72 *each* of pieces B, C, F, G, J, and K: Cut forty-five 1¼-inch strips. Refer to "Cutting Chart for Log Cabin Pieces" for lengths to cut the pieces from the strips.
- Twenty-four 1¼-inch strips for border strip sets

From the assorted light fabrics, cut:
- 68 *each* of pieces B, C, F, G, J, and K: Cut forty-two 1¼-inch strips. Refer to "Cutting Chart for Log Cabin Pieces" for lengths to cut the pieces from the strips.

CUTTING CHART FOR LOG CABIN PIECES

Begin with 1¼-inch strips. Cut assorted-length pieces from each fabric strip so that the fabric will be used in various locations in the blocks.

Piece	No. Cut from Fabric	Length of 1¼-inch Strip
B	72 medium, 68 light	2 inches
C	72 medium, 68 light	2¾ inches
D	140 dark	2¾ inches
E	140 dark	3½ inches
F	72 medium, 68 light	3½ inches
G	72 medium, 68 light	4¼ inches
H	140 dark	4¼ inches
I	140 dark	5 inches
J	72 medium, 68 light	5 inches
K	72 medium, 68 light	5¾ inches

Piecing the Log Cabin Units

You will need to make 140 Log Cabin units for the quilt. Sixty-eight of these use light-value fabrics for the light half of the unit. Seventy-two of the units use medium-value fabrics for the light half. The most efficient way to piece the units is to do the same step for all units of one type in assembly-line fashion. Make accurate ¼-inch seams when sewing. Press seam allowances away from the center square.

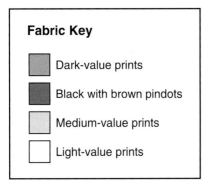

Fabric Key

■ Dark-value prints

■ Black with brown pindots

□ Medium-value prints

□ Light-value prints

1. Referring to the **Fabric Key,** begin by sewing a B strip to an A center square, as shown in **Diagram 1.** (The diagram shows light fabrics being used; remember that you need to make blocks with medium fabrics as well.)

Diagram 1

2. Sew a C strip to the long side of the Step 1 unit, as shown in **Diagram 2.**

Diagram 2

3. Referring to **Diagram 3,** continue to add lettered strips in order around the center until all eight strips have been added, forming a Log

Cabin unit. The completed units should measure 5¾ inches, including seam allowances. Repeat until you have 68 units made with light fabrics and 72 made with medium fabrics in the light portion of the unit.

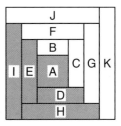

Diagram 3

Making the Full Blocks

1. Use two Log Cabin units with light fabrics and two units with medium fabrics to make each block. Lay out units as shown in the **Log Cabin Block Diagram,** paying careful attention to placement of light, medium, and dark areas.

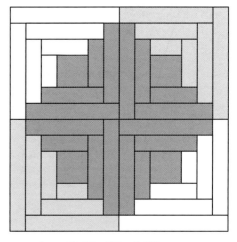

Log Cabin Block Diagram

2. Sew units together in two rows with two units in each row. Press seam allowances toward the blocks with light fabrics. Join the rows. Press seam allowance to one side. Repeat to make 24 blocks.

Making the Half-Blocks

1. Choose one Log Cabin unit with light fabrics and one unit with medium fabrics for each half-block.

2. Make ten half-blocks as in **Diagram 4A** and ten as in **Diagram 4B** by joining pairs of blocks. Press seam allowances to one side. You will have four Log Cabin units with medium fabrics left to use at the corners of the quilt top.

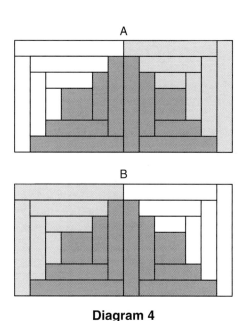

A

B

Diagram 4

Assembling the Inner Quilt Top

1. Referring to the **Quilt Diagram** and the photo on page 8, lay out the blocks, half-blocks, corner blocks, and sashing pieces in eight horizontal rows. Pay careful attention to the placement of the light and medium areas.

2. For the top and bottom rows, join corner blocks and half-blocks with short sashing strips between them. Press seam allowances toward the sashing strips.

3. To make the full-block rows, join half-blocks and blocks with sashing strips between them. Press seam allowances toward the sashing strips.

4. Measure the length of a row. Trim the long sashing strips to this length (approximately 56¾ inches).

5. Join the rows and sashing strips. Press seam allowances toward the sashing strips.

Making the Pieced Borders

1. Choose three dark strips and three medium strips for a strip set. Referring to **Diagram 5,** sew the six strips together, alternating medium and dark strips. Press seam allowances to one side. Make eight different strip sets.

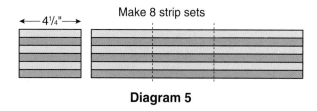

← 4¼" → Make 8 strip sets

Diagram 5

2. Cut a total of sixty-six 4¼-inch segments from the strip sets.

3. To make each side border, join 19 segments. Press seam allowances to one side.

4. To make the top and bottom border, join 14 segments for each border. Press seam allowances to one side.

Adding the Borders

1. Measure the length of the quilt top through the center. Trim two black borders to this length (approximately 79¼ inches). Sew borders to the sides of the quilt top. Press seam allowances toward the borders.

2. Measure the width of the quilt top through the center, including the side borders. Trim two black borders to this length (approximately 59¾ inches). Sew borders to the top and bottom edges of the quilt top. Press seam allowances toward the borders.

3. Pin a pieced border to the bottom edge of the quilt top. Leave five fabric strips extending beyond one edge of the black border. Sew the border to the quilt top, leaving approximately 6

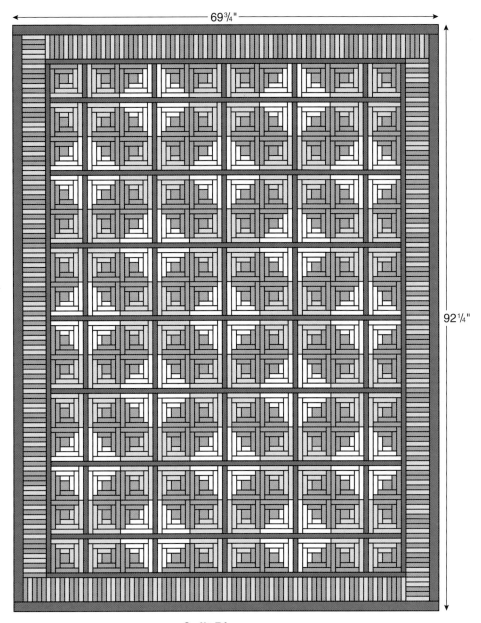

Quilt Diagram

inches unsewn at the end that extends beyond the black border **(Diagram 6A).** This seam will be finished after the other borders have been added. Press seam toward the black border.

4. See **Diagram 6B** for the order of adding borders. Pin a pieced border to the right side of

the quilt top. Position the border so it will be sewn to the short end of the bottom border. The opposite end of the side border should be even with the top edge of the top black border. Sew the border to the quilt, sewing the complete seam. Press seam allowance toward the black border.

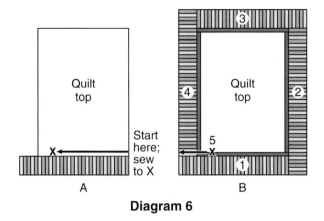

Diagram 6

5. In a similar manner, sew a pieced border to the top edge of the quilt and then to the left side, as shown in **Diagram 6B.**

6. Complete the seam on the bottom pieced border, sewing along the short end of the left side border.

7. Following the instructions in Steps 1 and 2, trim and sew black borders to the sides and then the top and bottom edges of the quilt top. Press seam allowances toward the black borders.

Quilting and Finishing

1. Mark quilting designs if desired. The quilt shown is machine quilted in the ditch along all sashing seams and along the black border edges. The blocks are randomly quilted with wavy lines to represent leaves blowing in the wind.

2. Divide the backing fabric into two 2¾-yard pieces. Divide one panel in half lengthwise. Sew a half panel to each long side of the full panel. Press the seam allowances away from the center panel.

3. Layer the quilt back, batting, and quilt top; baste. Trim the quilt back and batting so they are approximately 3 inches larger than the quilt top on all sides.

4. Hand or machine quilt as desired.

5. From the black fabric, make approximately 350 inches of French-fold binding. See page 164 for suggested binding widths and instructions on making and attaching binding.

6. Sew the binding to the quilt. Trim excess batting and backing, and hand-sew the folded edge of the binding to the wrong side of the quilt.

Yellow Monday

Quiltmaker: Elsie Moser

New York Beauty never looked so new! Splashy florals, traditional calicoes, and softly shaded hand-dyed fabrics combine in this spirited twist on a well-loved favorite. A lavishly appliquéd border adds the crowning touch to Elsie's arrestingly beautiful paper-pieced quilt.

Skill Level: Challenging

Size: Finished quilt is 75 inches square
Finished block is 15¼ inches square

Fabrics and Supplies

- ✓ 2 yards of yellow/purple large-scale floral print fabric for the blocks and borders
- ✓ 1¾ yards of dusty green print fabric for the blocks and borders
- ✓ 1⅛ yards of purple tone-on-tone striped fabric for the sashing and border strips
- ✓ ⅞ yard of olive green solid fabric for the vines and stems
- ✓ ⅞ yard of gold print fabric for the binding
- ✓ ¼ yard of fuchsia solid fabric for the corner squares in the blocks and borders
- ✓ Approximately 4 yards *total* of assorted purple, green, yellow, and gold print, hand-dyed and/or solid scraps for the blocks; each scrap should be 3 inches square, or larger
- ✓ Approximately 1 yard *total* of assorted purple and fuchsia scraps for the blocks and grape appliqués. Hand-dyed fabrics work beautifully, as do solids, and subtly textured, tone-on-tone prints.
- ✓ Approximately ½ yard *total* of assorted olive green print scraps for the leaf appliqués
- ✓ 4½ yards of fabric for the quilt back
- ✓ Full-size quilt batting (80 × 96 inches)
- ✓ Rotary cutter, ruler, and mat
- ✓ Template material
- ✓ Tracing paper or freezer paper for paper piecing
- ✓ Thread to match appliqué pieces

Cutting

The patterns for the leaf and grape appliqués on pages 23 and 24 do not require seam allowances. Add seam allowances as you cut each piece from fabric. Instructions are given for quick cutting the corner squares; sashing and border strips; and the A, B, and C strips with a rotary cutter and ruler. All of these measurements include ¼-inch seam allowances. Be aware that quick-cutting methods sometimes result in leftover pieces. Measurements for the borders are slightly longer than needed; trim them to the appropriate length when they are added to the quilt top.

Cut pieces in the following sequence:

From the yellow/purple floral, cut:
- Four 4¼ × 63-inch border strips
- 64 E pieces
- 4 J pieces

From the dusty green, cut:
- Four 2½ × 63-inch border strips
- 4 K pieces. The remaining fabric may be included in the green scrap fabric used for the blocks.

From the purple stripe, cut:
- Six 1¾ × 44-inch strips. Cut these strips into 1¾ × 14½-inch L strips. You will need a total of 12 L strips.
- Fourteen 1¾ × 44-inch strips. Cut these strips into 1¾ × 7½-inch G strips. You will need a total of 72 G strips; use leftovers from the previous step if necessary.

From the olive green solid, cut:
- One 30-inch square to be used for making continuous bias strips for the vines and stems

From the ¼ yard of fuchsia solid, cut:
- Two 1¾ × 44-inch strips. Cut these strips into 1¾-inch H corner squares. You will need a total of 32 H corner squares.
- 4 I pieces. The balance of this fabric can be used for grape appliqués.

From the assorted purple, green, yellow and gold scraps, cut:
- Three hundred eighty-four 1¾ × 3-inch A strips. Cut in sets of six strips, each from the same color but not necessarily the same fabric, for a total of 64 sets of six A strips each. "Look-alike" fabrics may be substituted if you run short of a specific fabric to complete a set.
- Three hundred twenty 2 × 3-inch B strips. Cut in sets of five strips, each from the same fabric, for a total of 64 sets of five B strips each.
- One hundred twenty-eight 1½ × 3-inch C strips. Cut two strips that match each set of B strips.

- 64 F pieces
- 64 F reverse pieces. These do not need to match the F pieces.
- 64 D pieces. Cut these from the purple and green scraps only.

From the assorted purple and fuchsia scraps, cut:
- 300 grapes, using the grape templates on page 56. You may cut equal numbers (75) of each size or any combination of sizes you like.

From the assorted olive green prints, cut:
- 19 small leaf appliqués
- 16 large leaf appliqués

Making the Paper Foundations

The pieced curved arc portions shown in the **Unit Diagram** are paper pieced. The remainder of these units are sewn without paper foundations. The finished blocks contain four of these units, for a total of 64 units and 16 finished blocks.

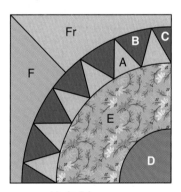

Unit Diagram

1. Make eight photocopies of the Paper Piecing Foundation Pattern on page 22. Be sure they are 100 percent accurate in size.

2. Layer eight sheets of tracing or freezer paper underneath one of the photocopied Paper Piecing Foundation Patterns and staple the edges together to hold them in place. Repeat this process for each of the remaining photocopies.

3. Using a short-to-medium stitch length and no thread on top or in the bobbin of the sewing machine, stitch over the seam lines of the pieced

arc as shown in **Diagram 1.** These needlepunched lines in the paper will become your sewing lines as you add fabric to the foundations. Working through the photocopy and the layers of tracing paper at the same time, cut out the foundation patterns along the solid lines.

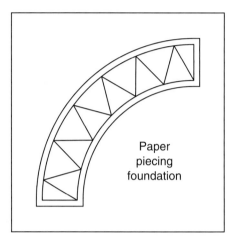

Diagram 1

Paper Piecing the Curved Arcs

For each unit, all A triangles should be from one or more similar fabrics in the same color family. All B and C triangles should be from a single fabric that contrasts strongly in color and/or value to the A pieces. Lay out several A, B, and C strips in various color combinations before sewing each pieced arc together. This will allow you to establish a balance of color and an effective contrast of value within the units.

1. Layer an A strip on top of a C strip, right sides together and position these strips underneath one of the paper piecing foundations, so that the C strip lies against the paper foundation, as shown in **Diagram 2.** The edges of the A and C strips must extend ¼ inch beyond the first seam line on the paper foundation, as shown. Starting and ending at the edges of the A and C strips, sew the first seam line (see the numbered seam line on the Paper Piecing Foundation Pattern for reference). Open up the A and C strips and press the seam flat.

2. Referring to **Diagram 3,** trim the edges of the opened A and C strips to ¼ inch beyond the second seam line.

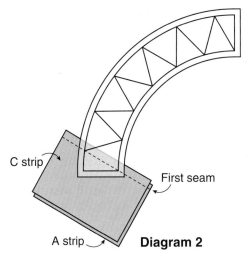

C strip

First seam

A strip

Diagram 2

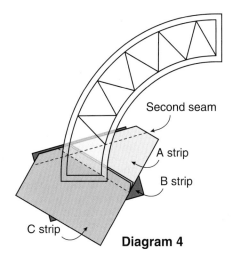

Second seam

A strip

B strip

C strip

Diagram 4

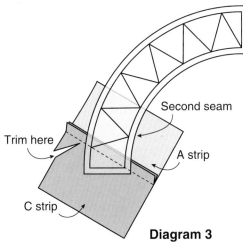

Second seam

Trim here

A strip

C strip

Diagram 3

Piecing the Blocks

The F and F reverse pieces should be of two different, contrasting fabrics.

1. Sew a D piece to an E piece as shown in **Diagram 5,** taking care to match midpoint markings and pin generously.

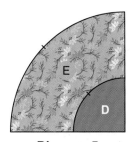

E

D

Diagram 5

2. Sew the combined D/E unit to the completed arc of A/B/C triangles, matching midpoints, as shown in **Diagram 6.**

3. Referring to **Diagram 4,** place a B strip right sides together with the A and C strips, matching the raw edges, as shown. Sew this second seam, open it up and press it flat. Trim the B strip to ¼ inch beyond the next seam.

4. In the same manner, continue sewing A and B strips in the numbered sequence shown on the Paper Piecing Foundation Pattern until there are five A strips, six B strips, and a final C strip on the tracing paper foundation. Press each seam flat as you go. This completes one pieced arc, as shown in the **Unit Diagram.**

5. Trim the edges of all A, B, and C strips even with the curved edges and the ends of the tracing paper foundation. Do not remove the tracing paper foundation at this time.

6. Repeat Steps 1 through 5 to make a total of 64 pieced arcs.

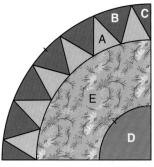

B

C

A

E

D

Diagram 6

3. Sew an F piece to an F reverse piece, as shown in **Diagram 7.**

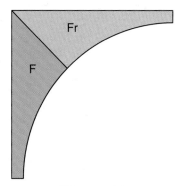

Diagram 7

4. Sew the F/F reverse unit to remaining portion of the unit, as shown in the **Unit Diagram** on page 16. As for any curved seam, take care to match midpoints and pin generously before sewing.

5. Repeat Steps 1 through 4 to make a total of 64 units.

Assembling the Blocks

Each block is composed of four pieced units, four G strips, and one H square. Refer to the **Block Diagram** and the photograph on page 14 for color guidance, and sew each block in the following sequence.

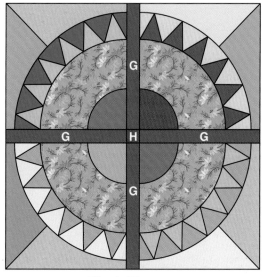

Block Diagram

1. Referring to the **Block Diagram,** sew one pieced unit to each side of a G strip. Press the seam allowances toward the G strip. Make two of these rows.

2. Referring to the **Block Diagram,** sew a G strip to each side of an H square and press the seam allowances toward the G strips.

3. Referring to the **Block Diagram,** sew the three parts of the block together, matching seams carefully. Since the seam allowances have been pressed in opposite directions, they should "nest" together well. Press the seam allowances toward the center G/H/G strip.

4. Make a total of 16 blocks.

Assembling the Quilt Top

1. Referring to the **Quilt Diagram,** lay out the 16 completed blocks in four rows of four blocks each. Arrange the blocks in the color balance that pleases you.

2. Referring to the **Quilt Diagram,** sew the blocks into four horizontal rows, pressing the seams allowances between blocks in opposite directions from row to row.

3. Referring to the **Quilt Diagram,** sew the four rows of blocks together, matching seams carefully. Press the seam allowances toward the top edge of the quilt top.

4. Use your thumbnail or the blunt end of a seam ripper to carefully remove the tracing paper foundations from the curved pieced arcs in each block.

Assembling the Borders

1. Sew a G strip to an H square, as shown in **Diagram 8.** Press the seam allowances away from the H square. Make eight G/H units.

Diagram 8

2. Sew together one L strip, an H square, an L strip, an H square, and another L strip, as shown in **Diagram 9.** Press all seam allowances away from the H squares. Make four L/H strips.

Quilt Diagram

3. Sew a short G/H strip to each end of the four long L/H strips, as shown in **Diagram 10.** Press the seam allowances away from the H squares, completing the four pieced border strips.

4. Crease the midpoint of one of the pieced border strips. Then crease the midpoint of one yellow/purple floral border strip and one dusty green border strip. Matching the midpoints, sew

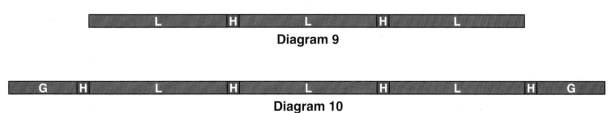

Diagram 9

Diagram 10

together the three border strips, as shown in the **Border Diagram.** Press all seam allowances toward the green border strip. Trim the floral and dusty green borders as necessary. Make four of these border units.

5. Crease the midpoints of the top and bottom edges of the quilt top. Matching midpoints and seams, sew a border unit to the top and bottom edges of the quilt top, referring to the **Quilt Diagram** on page 19. The pieced border lies closest to the center of the quilt top. Press the seam allowances toward the outer edges of the quilt.

6. Sew an I piece to a J piece, as shown in **Diagram 11,** taking care to match marked midpoints and pin generously. Press the seam allowance toward the I piece. Make four I/J units.

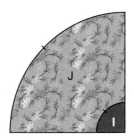

Diagram 11

7. Sew a K piece to an I/J unit, as shown in **Diagram 12,** matching and pinning carefully. Press the seam allowance toward the J piece. Make four of these corner block units.

8. Referring to the **Quilt Diagram,** sew a corner block unit to each end of the remaining two border units. Press the seam allowances toward the border units.

9. Crease the midpoint on both sides of the quilt top. Referring to the **Quilt Diagram,** sew a border unit to each side of the quilt top, matching seams carefully. Press the seam allowances toward the outer edges of the quilt.

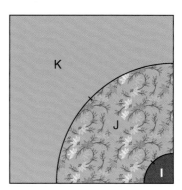

Diagram 12

Appliquéing the Borders

The appliqué borders in this quilt have a charming, free-form quality. There is no exact placement for each leaf or grape. Use your preferred method for preparing the leaves and grapes for appliqué. For more information on hand appliqué, see page 157.

1. Use the 30-inch square of olive green fabric to cut bias strips for the border vines and stems. Cut the bias strips 1⅜ inches wide. You'll need a length of 250 inches (approximately 7 yards) of bias strips sewn together to use for the vine; set the balance aside to use for the stems. The finished border vine should be approximately ½ inch wide. For more information on continuous bias strips, see page 158.

2. Using the quilt photograph on page 14 as a placement guide, pin the vine to the outer (floral/dusty green) border of the quilt top, trimming excess length if necessary.

3. Place and pin three small and four large leaf appliqués on each border, scattering a few extra leaves to casually overlap the inner borders. Use the remainder of the appliqués for the partial leaves along the edges of the quilt. Refer to the quilt photograph for guidance on leaf placement.

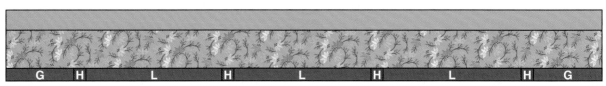

Border Diagram

INVISIBLE STOPS AND STARTS

To make the border vine appear to have no beginning or ending, arrange leaves and vines in a way that will allow you to hide the beginning and the end of the border vine strip underneath them. Once you are satisfied, hand baste the vine in place around the entire border.

4. Trim the remaining bias strips to a width of 1⅛ inches. Use bias bars to prepare a strip that finishes approximately ⅜ inch wide. Cut these strips into 35 stem segments that range from 1½ to 2 inches long. For more information on using bias bars, see page 158.

5. Connect the leaves to the vine by tucking the raw edges of a stem under both the leaf and the vine. Pin or baste the stems in place.

6. Appliqué the vine, leaves, and stems in place using a blind stitch and thread that matches the appliqué pieces. To avoid excess stretching of the bias strips, appliqué the inner curves of the vine first. Do not trim away the fabric behind the appliqué shapes in this quilt.

Tip: *Exception: If you choose the freezer paper appliqué method described on page 157, you'll need to remove the freezer paper.*★

7. Use the quilt photograph for assistance in placing the grapes along the vine. Grapes may be grouped in large and small bunches, with varying sizes in each bunch. The quilt shown has 76 grapes on the top border, 62 on the right, 89 on the bottom, and 73 on the left border, and no two clusters are exactly alike. Appliqué the grapes using a blind stitch and thread that matches the appliqué pieces.

Quilting and Finishing

1. Mark quilting designs as desired. The quilt shown is quilted in the ditch around pieces A through E, as shown in the **Block Quilting Diagram,** as well as around all sashing and appliqué shapes. The border vine is echo quilted at approximately 2-inch intervals through both the floral and dusty green borders.

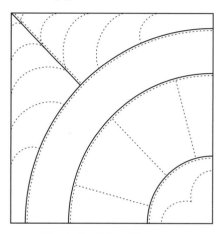

Block Quilting Diagram

2. To piece the quilt back, divide the backing fabric into two 2¼-yard pieces and remove the selvages. Divide one of the 2¼-yard pieces in half lengthwise, and sew each half to the long sides of the remaining full piece. Press the seams away from the center panel. The seams of the quilt back will lie parallel to the sides of the quilt.

3. Layer the quilt back, batting, and quilt top; baste. Trim the quilt back and batting 3 inches larger than the quilt top on all sides.

4. Quilt all marked designs, and add additional quilting if desired.

5. From the binding fabric, make approximately 310 inches of double-fold binding. For details on making and attaching binding, see page 164.

6. Sew the binding to the quilt top. Trim the excess batting and backing, and use matching thread and a blind stitch to hand-sew the folded edge of the binding to the back of the quilt.

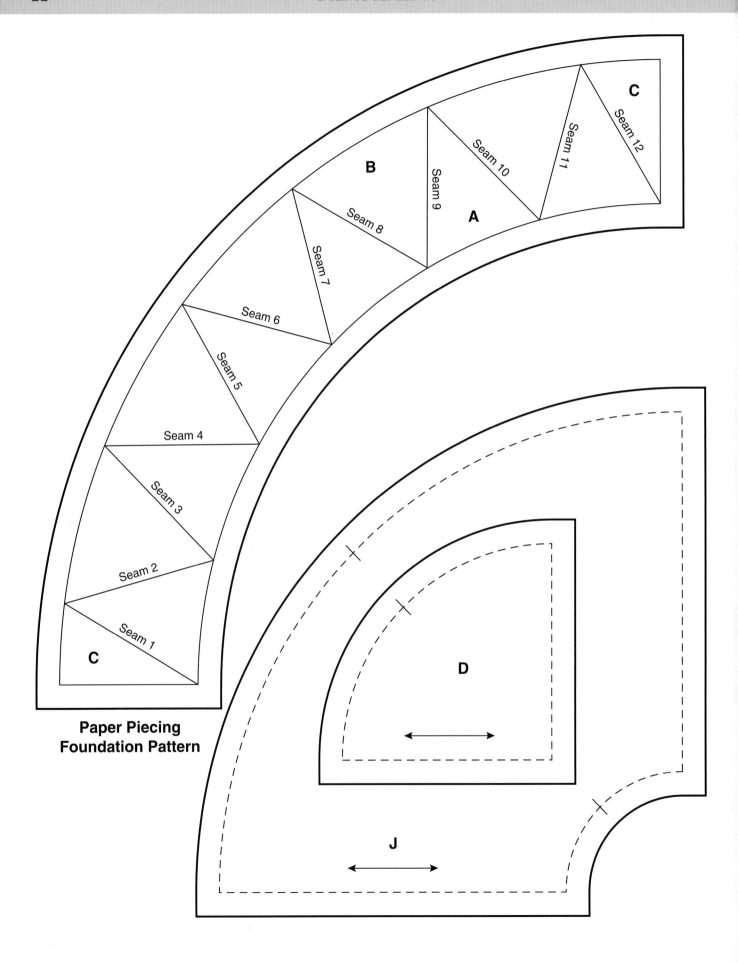

**Paper Piecing
Foundation Pattern**

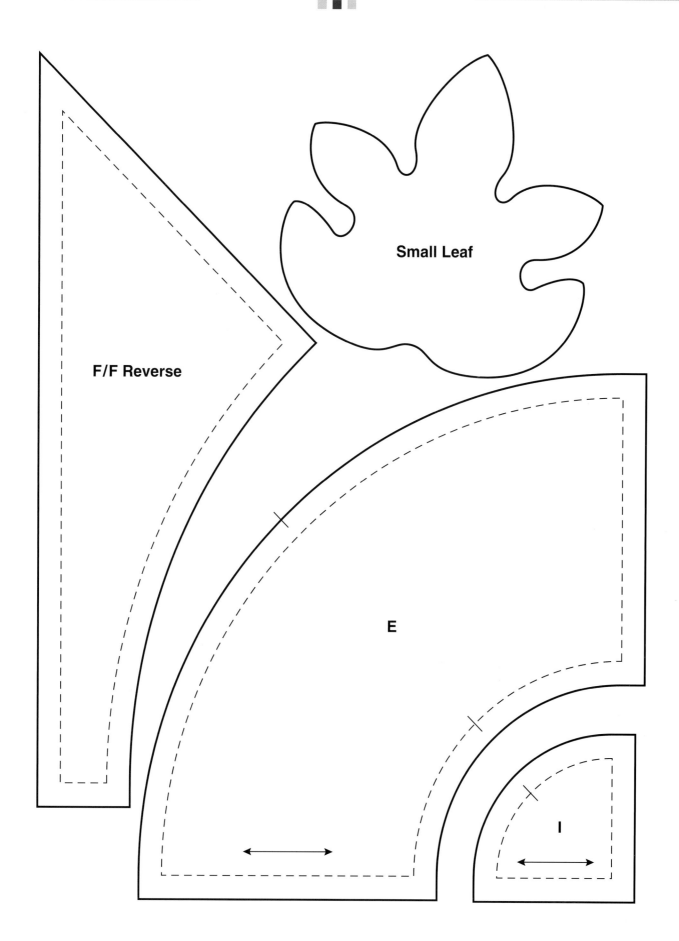

F/F Reverse

Small Leaf

E

I

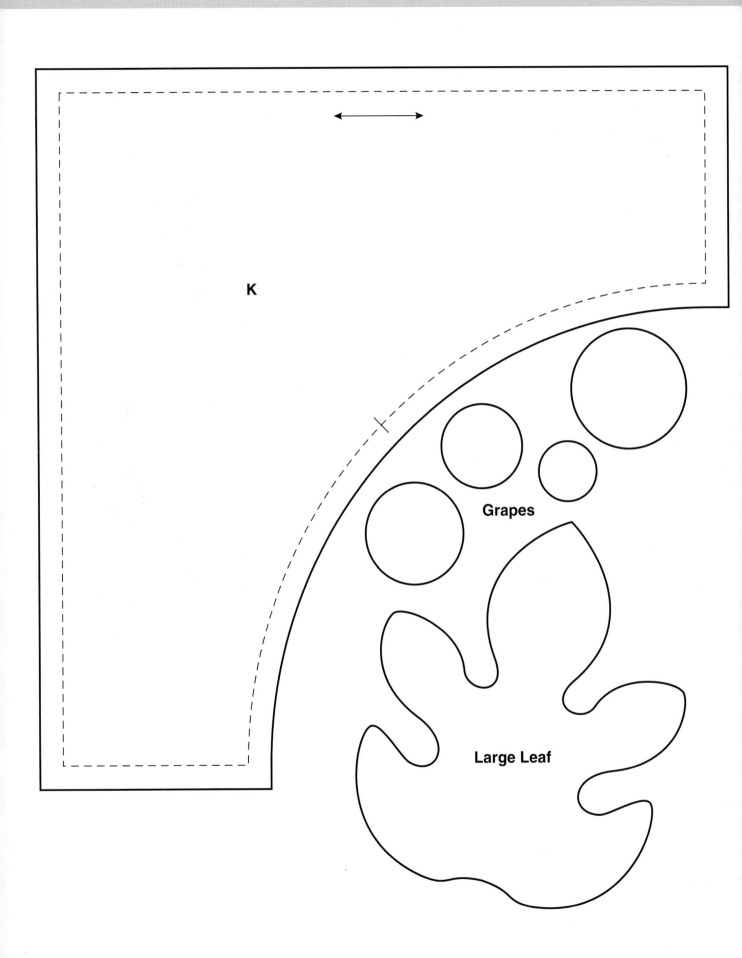

K

Grapes

Large Leaf

Basket Pillowcases

Quiltmaker: Sandra Barford

With pastel subtlety, Sandra created pillowcases that are as fresh as a spring breeze. The charming appliqué borders hint at flower beds and fresh buds, and the miniature basket blocks underline her garden theme. This pattern could easily be made into a wall quilt by continuing the appliqué border around all four edges.

Skill Level: Intermediate

Size: Finished pillowcase is approximately 20 × 30½ inches
Finished block is 6 inches square

Fabrics and Supplies for Two Pillowcases

✓ 1 yard of light print fabric for background, blocks, and borders

✓ ½ yard of pink print fabric for inner borders and binding

✓ ½ yard of green print fabric for the pieced sashing strips, appliquéd stems, and leaves

✓ Scraps (*each* approximately 8-inches square) of 24 different pastel print fabrics for the baskets and border appliqués

✓ 2 yards of white fabric for the pillowcase backings

✓ Template plastic

Cutting

All measurements include ¼-inch seam allowances. Measurements for the borders are longer than needed; trim them to the exact length when they are added to the pillowcase. Instructions are for quick-cutting the pieces with a rotary cutter and ruler. Note that for some of the pieces, quick-cutting and -piecing methods may result in leftovers or pieces that need to be trimmed.

From the light print fabric, cut:
- Two 5 × 22-inch strips for the appliqué borders
- Six 2 × 26-inch strips for the outer borders
- Twelve 3½-inch squares for the basket block centers
- Six 1½ × 44-inch strips for the pieced sashing strips
- Four 1⅜ × 44-inch strips. Cut these strips into 1⅜ × 3-inch D rectangles. You will need a total of 48 D rectangles.
- Two 2⅝ × 44-inch strips. Cut these strips into twenty-four 2⅝-inch squares; cut these squares in half diagonally to make 48 C triangles.

From the pink print fabric, cut:
- Eight 1½ × 25-inch strips for the inner borders
- Two 1½ × 44-inch binding strips

From the green print fabric, cut:
- Six 1½-inch × 44-inch strips for the pieced sashing strips
- 6 flower stems, using the H pattern on page 29
- 12 pieces for the leaves, using the G pattern on page 29

From each of the 24 pastel print fabric scraps, cut:
- One 3-inch square. Cut this square in half diagonally to make 2 A triangles.
- Two 1⅞-inch squares. Cut these squares in half diagonally to make 4 B triangles.
- Two 1⅛ × 3½-inch bias strips for the basket handles
- 6 different groups of 4 F pieces from 6 of the pastels for the flower petals
- 6 E pieces from yellow prints for the flower centers

From the white fabric, cut:
- Two 24 × 34-inch pieces for the pillowcase backings

Appliquéing the Handles

1. Lay a 3½-inch basket block center square over the Handle Placement Diagram on page 29. With a pencil, mark light placement lines for the basket handles. Repeat for each basket block center square.

2. Lay four pastel print A triangles around each basket block center square, using the photograph on page 25 as a guide to color placement, or experiment until you have an arrangement that pleases you.

3. Fold one 1⅛ × 3½-inch bias handle strip in half lengthwise, wrong sides together. Sew ¼ inch from the fold and trim the seam allowance to ⅛ inch. Press the strip flat, with the pressed seam allowance underneath. Shape a curve into the handle strip to prepare it for appliqué. The prepared strip will be approximately ¼ inch wide.

4. Baste the handle strip along the marked curve on a center square. Appliqué with a blind stitch, doing the inner curve first and then the outer curve, to make the handle lie flat. Remove the basting thread and repeat for the remaining handle strips on each center block. Refer to page 157 for more information on hand appliqué.

Piecing the Blocks

1. Sew A triangles to each side of a basket block center, as shown in **Diagram 1,** matching the fabric of each A triangle to the appliquéd handles. Press the seams toward the A triangles. Repeat for all basket block centers.

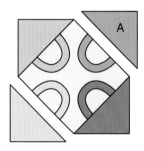

Diagram 1

2. Sew a B triangle to each end of a D rectangle, as shown in **Diagram 2.** Referring to **Diagram 1,** match the fabric of the B triangles to the appropriate basket bases in the basket block centers. Press the seams toward the B triangles. Repeat for all D rectangles.

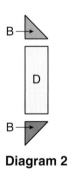

Diagram 2

3. Referring to **Diagram 3,** sew B/D strips to the appropriate sides of each basket block center. Press the seams toward the B/D strips.

4. Sew C triangles to the corners of each basket block, as shown in **Diagram 4.** Press the seams toward the C triangles. You will have a total of 12 basket blocks.

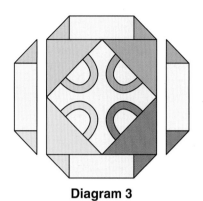

Diagram 3

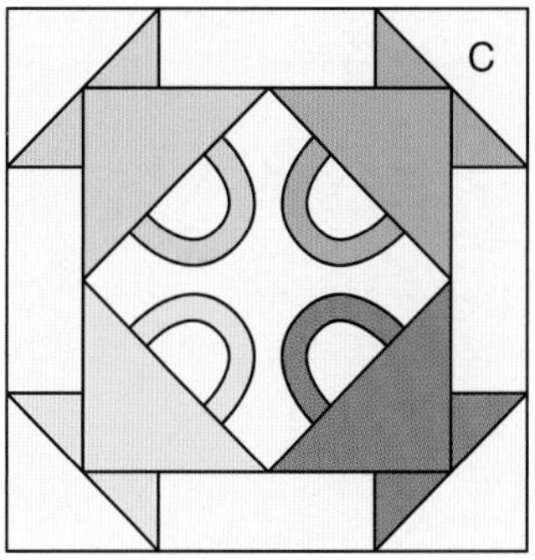

Diagram 4

Appliquéing the Border

1. Transfer the Flower Appliqué Motif on page 17 to each 5 × 22-inch appliqué border strip with a pencil. Position the pieces for each motif approximately 2 inches apart on each border and reverse the direction of the center flower, referring to the **Pillowcase Top Diagram** on page 28 as a placement guide.

2. Appliqué pieces E, F, G and H in place with a blind stitch.

Piecing the Sashing

1. Sew two 1½-inch green strips and one light print strip together into a strip set, as shown in **Diagram 5** on page 28. Press the seams toward the green fabric. Make a total of two of these strip sets. Sew two 1½-inch light print strips and one green strip together, as shown in **Diagram 5,** to make a second strip set. Press the seams toward the light print fabric. Repeat to make a total of two of these strip sets.

Pillowcase Top Diagram

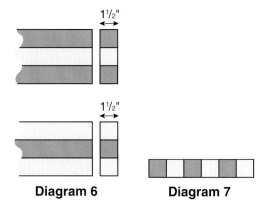

1½"

1½"

Diagram 6   **Diagram 7**

4. Alternating colors, sew eight segments together end to end to make a long sashing strip, as shown in **Diagram 8.** Make a total of six long sashing strips. Note that each will be trimmed when you add it to the pillowcase top.

Diagram 8

Assembling the Pillowcase Top

1. Referring to the **Pillowcase Top Diagram** for placement of blocks and colors in sashing strips, lay the blocks out in two vertical rows of three blocks each. Place a short sashing strip between each block as well as at the top and bottom edges of the blocks.

2. Referring to the **Pillowcase Top Diagram** for color placement, place long sashing strips between and at the sides of the rows of blocks. Remove the two unneeded squares from each long sashing strip after determining the correct color placement.

3. Sew the blocks and the short sashing strips together into vertical rows. Press the seams toward the sashing strips.

4. Sew the long sashing strips to the vertical rows of blocks. Press the seams toward the sashing strips.

5. Measure the length of the pillowcase top. Trim two 1½ × 25-inch pink print inner borders to this measurement and sew them to the side edges. Press the seams toward the border.

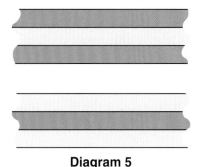

Diagram 5

2. Cut each of the strip sets into 1½-inch segments, as shown in **Diagram 6.** You will need a total of 40 segments from each color combination.

3. Alternating colors, sew two segments together end to end to make a short sashing strip, as shown in **Diagram 7.** Make a total of 16 short sashing strips.

6. Measure the width of the pillowcase top, including the borders. Trim the remaining two pink inner border strips to this measurement and sew them to the top and bottom edges of the pillowcase top. Press the seams toward the borders.

7. In the same manner, sew the 2 × 26-inch light print outer borders to the side edges and press the seams toward the borders. Sew the remaining two outer border strip to one end and the appliqué border to the other. Press the seams toward the borders.

8. Repeat Steps 1 through 7 to assemble the second pillowcase top.

Finishing

1. Trim the pieces of white backing fabric to match the size of each completed pillowcase top.

2. Pin the pillowcase top and the backing right sides together. Sew along two sides and one end, using a ¼-inch seam allowance. Leave the appliqué border end open. Turn the pillowcase right side out and press.

3. Make 90 inches of double-fold binding from the pink print fabric. Bind the border edge of the pillowcase and sew the binding to the wrong side with a blind stitch. For more instructions on making and attaching binding, see page 164.

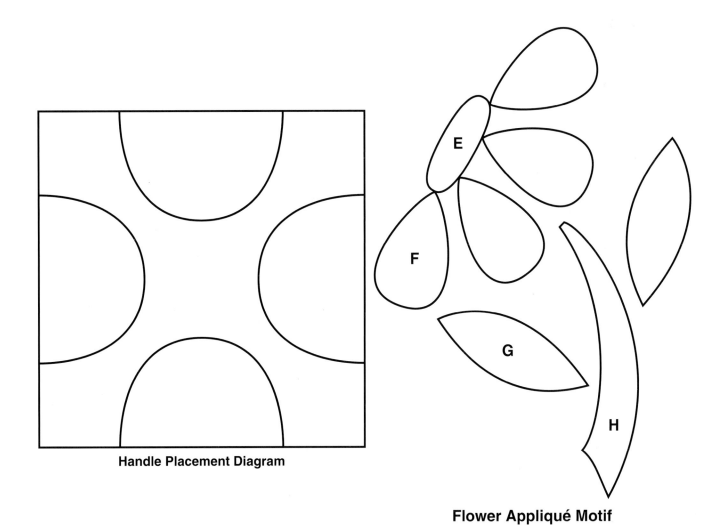

Handle Placement Diagram

Flower Appliqué Motif

Thanksgiving Wall Quilt

Quiltmaker: Kathy Berschneider

Kathy searched everywhere to find the perfect fabrics for her autumn wall quilt. After visiting all of the stores near her home in Rockford, Illinois, she finally found the focal print she wanted in Sun Prairie, Wisconsin. With a Thanksgiving theme in mind, she selected warm autumn tones for the Indian Trails blocks, although in different colors, this pattern would also make a nice quilt for other holidays.

Skill Level: Easy

Size: Finished quilt is 31 × 31 inches
Finished block is 6 inches square

Fabrics and Supplies

NOTE: A multicolored focal fabric is an interesting, medium- to large-scale print.

- ✓ ¾ yard of focal fabric for the blocks
- ✓ ¼ yard of focal or other fabric for the binding
- ✓ ⅝ yard of teal print for the blocks
- ✓ ½ yard of light orange print for the blocks
- ✓ ½ yard of orange plaid for the blocks
- ✓ 1 yard of muslin for the quilt back
- ✓ Crib-size batting (45 × 60 inches)

Cutting

This quilt is quick cut using a rotary cutter and ruler, without templates. All measurements include ¼-inch seam allowances.

From the focal fabric, cut:
- Four 2¼ × 44-inch border strips
- Two 5¾ × 44-inch strips. Cut these strips into eight 5⅜-inch squares; cut these squares in half diagonally to make 16 triangles.

From the orange plaid, cut:
- Two 5¾ × 44-inch strips. Cut these strips into eight 5⅜-inch squares; cut these squares in half diagonally to make 16 triangles.

From the teal print, cut:
- Four 1¾ × 44-inch border strips
- Three 2⅜ × 44-inch strips. Cut these strips into forty-eight 2⅜-inch squares; cut these squares in half diagonally to make 96 triangles.

From the light orange print, cut:
- Three 2⅜ × 44-inch strips. Cut these strips into forty-eight 2⅜-inch squares; cut these squares in half diagonally to make 96 triangles.
- One 2 × 44-inch strip. Cut strip into 2-inch squares. You will need a total of 16 squares; do not cut these squares in half.

Piecing the Blocks

1. Stitch a teal triangle to a light orange triangle, as shown in **Diagram 1.** Press the seams toward the light orange triangle. Make 96 triangle-pieced squares.

2. Sew three teal and light orange triangle-pieced squares together, as shown in **Diagram 2,** forming the green points for one side of the block.

Diagram 1   **Diagram 2**

3. Sew a 2-inch light orange square to one end of this row, as shown in **Diagram 3.** Make 16 of these rows for the right side of the block.

4. Sew together a row of three triangle-pieced squares for the left side of the block, reversing the positions of the colors, as shown in **Diagram 4.**

Diagram 3   **Diagram 4**

5. Sew the large focal print triangles to the plaid triangles, as shown in the **Block Diagram.**

Block Diagram

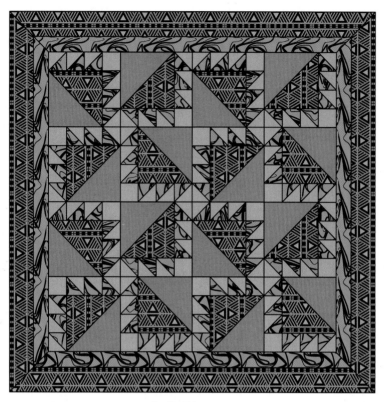

Quilt Diagram

6. Referring to the **Block Diagram,** sew the shorter row of triangle-pieced squares to the side of the large focal print and plaid triangle-pieced square. Press the seams toward the focal print. Sew the longer row of triangle-pieced squares to the other side of the large triangle-pieced square. Make a total of 16 blocks.

Assembling the Quilt Top

Lay the blocks out in four rows of four blocks, as shown in the **Quilt Diagram.** Sew the blocks together into four rows. Press the seams in alternate directions. Sew the rows of blocks together. Press the seams in opposite directions.

Adding the Borders

1. Sew the teal border strips to the focal fabric border strips. The border pieces will be longer than necessary and will be trimmed later.

2. Sew the top and bottom borders to the quilt top, starting and stopping ¼ inch in from the edges of the quilt top. Do not press these seams. Repeat this process with the side borders.

3. Miter the corners of the borders. For instructions on mitering corners, see page 160.

Quilting and Finishing

1. Mark the quilt top for quilting. Kathy elected to quilt in the ditch around individual pieces so no marking was necessary.

2. Layer the quilt back, batting, and quilt top; baste. Trim the quilt back and batting so they are approximately 3 inches larger than the quilt top on all sides. Quilt as desired.

3. From the binding fabric, make approximately 130 inches of double-fold binding. See page 164 for suggested binding widths and instructions on making and attaching binding.

4. Sew the binding to the quilt top. Trim the excess batting and backing, and hand-sew the folded edge of the binding to the back of the quilt.

5. To make a sleeve to hang your finished wallhanging, hem the short ends of an 8½ × 31-inch strip of fabric and sew it into a tube. Hand stitch the sleeve to the upper back edge of the quilt. For more instructions on making a hanging sleeve, see page 166.

Scrap Baskets

Quiltmaker: Kris Merkens

Small amounts of many different scrap fabrics are featured in this delightful wallhanging. Kris combined a fondness for the basket pattern with her favorite color, blue, to create a small quilt with a real country feeling. Our quick-cutting and piecing instructions will help you put this little quilt together in record time.

Skill Level: Intermediate to Challenging (The patchwork pieces are tiny, so seam allowances must be exact in order to construct this quilt.)

Size: Finished quilt is 28¾ × 34¾ inches. Finished block is 4 inches square

Fabrics and Supplies

- ✓ 1 yard of dark blue print fabric for borders and binding
- ✓ ½ yard of cream print fabric for pieced border
- ✓ ¼ yard each of three different cream and beige print fabrics for setting triangles and block backgrounds
- ✓ ⅛ yard of nine assorted medium to dark print fabrics for basket tops and bottoms and pieced border*
- ✓ 1 yard of fabric for quilt back
- ✓ Crib-size quilt batting (45 × 60 inches)
- ✓ Rotary cutter, ruler, and mat

* Cut pieces from a larger assortment of fabrics if you would like a scrappier quilt. The colors used in the quilt shown are various dark and medium blues, reds, greens, and browns.

Cutting

All measurements include ¼-inch seam allowances. Measurements for the borders are longer than needed; trim them to the exact length when they are added to the quilt top. Instructions are given for quick-cutting the pieces with a rotary cutter and ruler.

From the dark blue print fabric, cut:
- Four 3¼ × 44-inch outer border strips
- One 1⅞ × 44-inch inner border strip
- Two 1½ × 44-inch inner border strips
- Reserve the remaining fabric for binding

From the cream print border fabric, cut:
- Two 3⅜ × 44-inch strips. From the strips, cut twenty-one 3⅜-inch squares. Cut each square in half diagonally in both directions to make a total of eighty-four F setting triangles.

- One 2 × 44-inch strip. From the strip, cut eight 2-inch squares. Cut each square in half once diagonally to make a total of sixteen G corner triangles.

From each of the three cream and beige fabrics, cut:
- One 7-inch square. Cut each of the three squares in half diagonally in both directions to make a total of twelve H setting triangles. Two will not be used.
- One 3¾-inch square from two of the background fabrics. Cut each square in half once diagonally to make four I corner triangles.
- One 1⅞-inch × 44-inch strip. Cut eighteen 1⅞-inch squares from each strip, or a total of fifty-four squares for block backgrounds.
- One 1½-inch × 28-inch strip. Cut twelve 1½-inch B squares from each strip for block backgrounds.
- Three 2⅞-inch squares for block backgrounds, or a total of nine squares.
- One 1½-inch × 44-inch strip. Cut twelve 1½-inch × 2½-inch D background rectangles from each strip.

From each of the 9 assorted print fabrics, cut:
- One 2⅞-inch square for baskets, or a total of nine squares.
- Two 1⅞-inch squares for basket bases, or a total of eighteen squares.
- Two 1⅞-inch squares for basket handles, or a total of eighteen squares. (Or cut the same number of squares from a wider variety of fabrics for a scrappier look.)
- One 2 × 12-inch strip. Cut five 2-inch E border squares from each strip. Cut one more 2-inch square from any print to equal a total of forty-six squares.

Assembling the Triangle Units

1. Referring to **Diagram 1**, draw a diagonal line from one corner to another on the reverse side of each cream or beige 1⅞-inch background square. Repeat for the nine 2⅞-inch cream background squares.

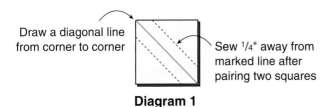

Draw a diagonal line from corner to corner

Sew 1/4" away from marked line after pairing two squares

Diagram 1

2. To make A basket base units, pair a 1⅞-inch background square with a basket base square of the same size, right sides together and edges matched.

3. Sew each pair together with two seams, each ¼ inch from the marked line, as shown in **Diagram 1**. If you don't have a ¼-inch presser foot, draw the seam lines, too, before beginning.

4. Use scissors or rotary cutting equipment to cut through both layers of squares on the marked line.

5. Place the thirty-six new units on your ironing board, dark triangle up. You'll need to take great care not to distort or stretch the units as you press the seams: *Before* you open up the unit, press a medium-hot iron onto each sewn unit at the seam line, "setting" the seam as it was sewn. Open a unit by flipping up the dark triangle, making sure the seam allowance is towards the dark fabric, as shown in **Diagram 2**. Carefully move the iron into the diagonal seam line that separates the dark half from the light half, pressing by lifting the iron with an up and down motion and not by sliding the iron along the seamline. Open up and press all units, as shown in the diagram. Trim away the seam allowance nubs at two corners.

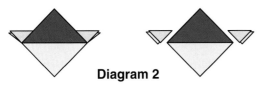

Diagram 2

6. To make C units for baskets, pair each 2⅞-inch basket base square with a background square of the same size. Sew, cut, and press as for A basket base units, assembling eighteen square units. Set aside with matching bases.

7. To make A units for basket handles, pair each remaining 1⅞-inch dark square with a background square of the same size. Assemble as before to make basket handle units. Keep units with like backgrounds together.

Piecing the Blocks

1. Referring to **Diagram 3**, lay out the A, B, C, and D units for one block. Use matching cream or beige print pieces in the background area and matching colored pieces for the basket and base portion of the block. Use other print combinations of A triangle units for the handle portion of the basket.

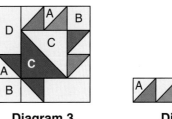

Diagram 3

Diagram 4

2. Sew the A handle squares together in pairs, as shown in **Diagram 4**. Press seams toward the darker fabrics whenever possible.

3. Referring to **Diagram 5** for correct placement, sew a pair of A pieced squares to one side of the C pieced square.

4. Add a B square to the remaining pair of A pieced squares to make a strip, paying attention to placement. Sew the strip to the side of the Step 3 unit.

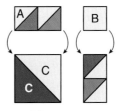

Diagram 5

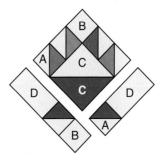

Diagram 6

5. Referring to **Diagram 6**, sew each base A pieced square to a D rectangle.

6. Sew one AD strip to the lower right side of the block, as shown in **Diagram 6**. Sew the remaining B square to the end of the remaining AD strip. Sew the strip to the lower left side of the block to complete it.

7. Repeat to make a total of 18 blocks.

Assembling the Quilt Top

1. Referring to the **Quilt Diagram**, lay out the 18 pieced blocks, the H side setting triangles, and the I corner setting triangles.

2. Join the blocks and setting pieces in diagonal rows. Press the seams in opposite directions from row to row.

3. Join the rows to complete the inner quilt.

Adding the Borders

1. Measure the width of the quilt (approximately 17⅜ inches). Cut two inner border strips to length from the 1⅛-inch-wide dark blue strip. Sew the borders to the top and bottom of the quilt.

2. Measure the length of the quilt (approximately 25¾ inches). Cut the 1½-inch-wide dark blue inner border strips to length, and sew them to the sides of the quilt top.

3. To make the pieced border, sew cream print F triangles to opposite sides of 38 E border squares, as shown in **Diagram 7**.

4. Sew F and G triangles to the eight remaining E squares to make eight corner units, as shown in **Diagram 8**.

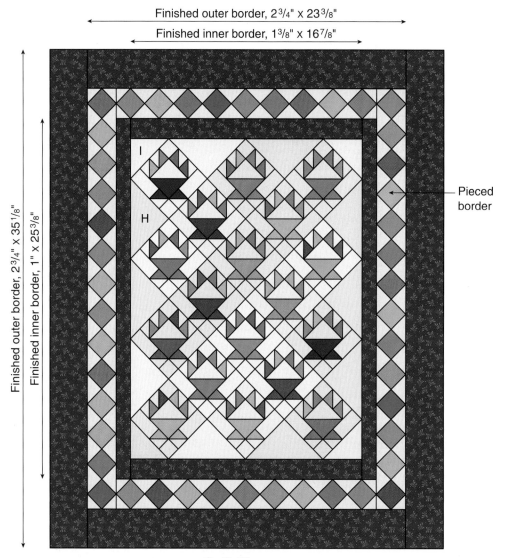

Finished outer border, 2¾" x 23⅜"

Finished inner border, 1⅜" x 16⅞"

Finished outer border, 2¾" x 35⅛"

Finished inner border, 1" x 25⅜"

Pieced border

Quilt Diagram

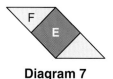

Diagram 7

Diagram 8

5. Make each top and bottom pieced border by joining seven Step 3 units together to make a strip. Add a Step 4 corner unit to each end of the strip. Sew the pieced borders to the top and bottom of the inner quilt top. Press the seams toward the blue inner borders.

6. Make each side pieced border by joining 12 Step 3 units together to make a strip, and add a Step 4 corner unit to each end. Sew the borders to the sides of the quilt top. Press the seams toward the blue borders.

7. Measure the width of the quilt top (approximately 23⅞ inches). Trim two 3¼-inch-wide dark blue print outer border strips to the width of the quilt. Sew the borders to the top and bottom of the quilt top. Press the seams toward the borders.

8. Measure the length of the quilt top (approximately 35¾ inches). Trim the two remaining 3¼-inch-wide outer border strips to the length of the quilt. Sew the strips to the sides of the quilt top. Press the seams toward the borders.

Quilting and Finishing

1. Mark quilting designs. The quilting patterns for the H side and I corner setting triangles are given below.

2. Layer the quilt back, batting, and quilt top; baste. Trim the quilt back so it is approximately 3 inches larger than the quilt top on all sides.

3. Quilt all marked designs. Add additional quilting as desired. On the quilt shown, the basket blocks and the pieced border have quilting in the ditch along the seams. A square grid is quilted in the border.

4. From the reserved binding fabric, make approximately 140 inches of double-fold binding. See page 164 for suggested binding widths and instructions on making and attaching binding.

5. Sew the binding to the quilt top. Trim the excess batting and backing, and hand-sew the folded edge of the binding to the back of the quilt. Add a hanging sleeve to the back. Refer to page 166 for instructions on making and adding a hanging sleeve.

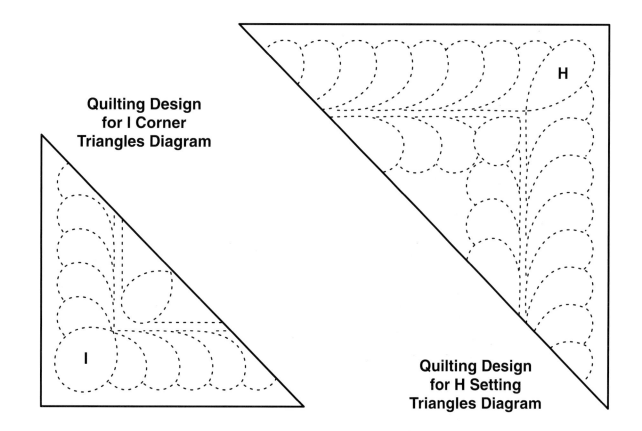

Quilting Design for I Corner Triangles Diagram

Quilting Design for H Setting Triangles Diagram

Country Casuals

August
Jim's Scrappy Nine Patch
Old Schoolhouse
Brick Wall
Patchwork Pillows

■

August

Quiltmaker: Norma Grasse

When Norma drew the month of August in her group's "Calendar Quilt Challenge," she knew exactly what she wanted to do. This original design combines two of her favorite things—sunflowers and birds—in a whimsical blend of piecework and appliqué. The result is as fresh and upbeat as a late summer morning.

Skill Level: Challenging

Size: Finished quilt is 95 inches square
Finished block size is 12 inches square

Fabrics and Supplies

- ✓ 6 yards of unbleached muslin for the blocks and borders
- ✓ 3¾ yards of medium gold print fabric for the blocks, appliqués, and binding
- ✓ 2½ yards of medium green solid fabric for the bias vines and stems
- ✓ 2 yards of green small-scale floral print fabric for the sashing strips
- ✓ 2 yards of dark brown swirly print fabric for the sunflower centers
- ✓ ⅔ yard of black sprigged print fabric for the rooster appliqués
- ✓ ⅔ yard of green check print fabric for the rooster appliqués
- ✓ ⅔ yard of green and red swirly print fabric for the rooster appliqués
- ✓ ⅔ yard of brown feathery print fabric for the rooster appliqués
- ✓ ½ yard of a light gold feathery print fabric for the blocks and appliqués
- ✓ ⅓ yard of medium red dotted fabric for the rooster appliqués
- ✓ 8⅝ yards of fabric for the quilt back
- ✓ King-size batting (120 inches square)
- ✓ Rotary cutter, ruler, and mat
- ✓ 12½-inch square of tracing paper
- ✓ Black permanent marking pen
- ✓ Water-soluble marker or mechanical pencil
- ✓ Template material
- ✓ Thread to match the appliqué fabrics
- ✓ Black embroidery floss
- ✓ Embroidery needle

Cutting

Instructions are for quick cutting the background squares, bias vines and stems, sashing strips, and borders with a rotary cutter and ruler. These measurements include ¼-inch seam allowances.

Full-size patterns for all other pieces appear on pages 47–50. Transfer these patterns to template material. For instructions for making and using templates, see page 153.

Pattern pieces A, B, C, and D include ¼-inch seam allowances. If you prefer to piece the sunflower block by hand, do not include this seam allowance in the template. For hand piecing, the actual seamlines are traced onto the fabric and the seam allowances are added when cutting out each piece from the fabric.

Appliqué pieces do not include seam allowances. To cut the R-1 through R-13 pieces in reversed positions, simply flip each of these templates to the reverse side before placing it on the fabric. You may find it helpful to keep two piles of rooster fabric pieces, labeling one stack "reverse." Follow the same procedure for cutting pieces L-1 through L-3 reverse. Cut pieces in the following order:

From the unbleached muslin, cut:
- Four 13½ × 72-inch border strips
- Twelve 12½-inch square blocks
- Four 11½-inch square blocks
- 52 D pieces
- 208 C pieces

From the medium gold print, cut:
- 44 S-1 sunflower appliqués
- 208 B diamonds
- 8 R-7 and 8 R-7 reverse rooster foot appliqués
- Reserve the remaining fabric for the binding

From the medium green solid, cut:
- One 42-inch square for continuous bias vines and stems
- 8 L-1 leaf and 8 L-1 reverse leaf appliqués
- 8 L-2 leaf and 9 L-2 reverse leaf appliqués
- 19 L-3 leaf and 20 L-3 reverse leaf appliqués

From the green floral print, cut:
- Three 1½ × 72-inch strips. Cut these strips into eight 1½ × 13½-inch-long segments and eight 1½ × 11½-inch-long segments.

- Two 2 × 69½-inch sashing strips for the top and bottom sashing strips
- Six 2 × 66½-inch vertical sashing strips
- Four 2 × 63-inch strips. Cut these strips into 2 × 12½-inch sashing strips. You will need a total of 20 sashing strips.

From the dark brown swirly print, cut:
- 13 E circles for the sunflower centers in the blocks
- 44 S-2 circles for the sunflower centers in the borders

From the black sprigged print, cut:
- 8 R-2 and 8 R-2 reverse tail feather appliqués
- 8 R-4 and 8 R-4 reverse tail feather appliqués
- 8 R-6 and 8 R-6 reverse tail feather appliqués

From the green check fabric, cut:
- 8 R-1 and 8 R-1 reverse tail feather appliqués
- 8 R-3 and 8 R-3 reverse tail feather appliqués
- 8 R-5 and 8 R-5 reverse tail feather appliqués

From the red swirly print, cut:
- 8 R-8 and 8 R-8 reverse rooster chest appliqués

From the green swirly print, cut:
- 8 R-9 and 8 R-9 reverse rooster chest appliqués

From the brown feathery print, cut:
- 8 R-10 and 8 R-10 reverse rooster chest appliqués

From the light gold feathery print, cut:
- 208 A triangles
- 8 R-12 and 8 R-12 reverse rooster head appliqués

From the medium red dotted fabric, cut:
- 8 R-11 and 8 R-11 reverse rooster comb appliqués
- 8 R-13 and 8 R-13 reverse rooster comb appliqués

Piecing the Sunflower Blocks

This quilt consists of 13 pieced sunflower blocks, each with an appliquéd center circle.

1. Referring to the **Sunflower Block Diagram,** lay out 16 A triangles, 16 B diamonds, 16 C triangles, four D pieces, and one E center circle.

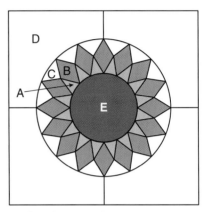

Sunflower Block Diagram

2. Sew an A triangle to a B diamond, stopping the seam ¼ inch in from the raw edge, as indicated by the dot in **Diagram 1,** to allow the subsequent C pieces to be set in easily at an angle. Make 16 of these A/B units.

Diagram 1

3. Referring to **Diagram 2,** sew these A/B units into groups of four, followed by groups of eight, and finally into the 16 units that complete the pieced portion of the sunflower. Press the seam allowances toward the A triangles.

Diagram 2

4. Insert a C piece between the points of the B diamonds, as shown in **Diagram 3.** Sew from the pivot point out to the edge of the B diamonds. Press the seam allowances toward the C pieces.

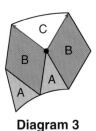

Diagram 3

5. Prepare the E center circle for hand appliqué and pin it over the center of the pieced sunflower, as shown in **Diagram 4.** Appliqué it with a blind stitch.

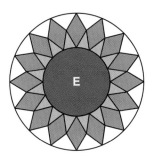

Diagram 4

6. Fold each of the D pieces in half and crease the midpoints. Match these midpoints to center B diamond in each quarter of the sunflower. Sew a D piece to each quarter, leaving a ¼ inch free at each end, as shown in **Diagram 5,** in order to complete the remaining short side seams easily. Press these seam allowances toward the D pieces.

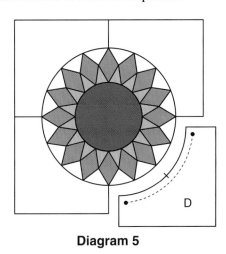

Diagram 5

7. Referring to **Diagram 5,** complete the sunflower block by sewing the remaining short side seams of the D pieces. Press these seam allowances to one side.

8. Make a total of 13 sunflower blocks.

Appliquéing the Rooster Blocks

There are twelve 12-inch appliquéd rooster blocks in the center of this quilt top. There are also four 11-inch rooster blocks at the corners of the quilt borders. Prepare and appliqué the blocks in the same manner; only the size of the muslin background square differs.

Study the quilt photograph on page 40. You will notice that in half of the blocks, the roosters face toward the right and in the other half the roosters face toward the left. In eight of the blocks, you will use pattern pieces R-1 through R-13. For the other eight blocks, use pieces R-1 reverse through R-13 reverse.

1. To make a master pattern for marking the appliqué design on the background squares, fold a 12½-inch square of tracing paper in half vertically, horizontally, and diagonally in both directions. Referring to the **Rooster Block Diagram** for the correct placement of each appliqué shape, use the appliqué templates and a mechanical pencil to draw the outlines of the rooster on the tracing paper, remembering that some of the

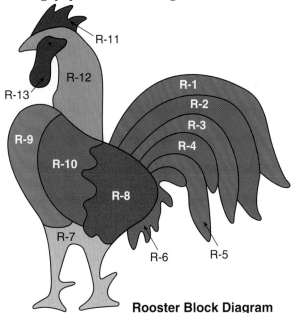

Rooster Block Diagram

pieces will overlap each other when they are stitched. When you are satisfied with the master pattern, darken the drawn lines with a black permanent marking pen and allow the ink to dry.

2. Referring to the **Rooster Block Diagram** on page 43, prepare pieces R-1 through R-13 according to your preferred method for hand appliqué.

3. Fold and lightly crease a 12½-inch background square in half vertically, horizontally, and diagonally in both directions.

4. Center the background square over the master pattern. Using a water-soluable fabric pen or a mechanical pencil, lightly transfer the pattern guidelines to the background square.

5. Referring to the **Rooster Block Diagram,** position, baste and appliqué the rooster in numerical order, beginning with R-1 and working through R-13. Note that there is no need to appliqué a seam allowance where another piece will overlap it. For more information on hand appliqué, see page 157.

6. Using three or four strands of black embroidery floss, embroider an eye on each rooster, using either a French knot or a satin stitched circle.

7. Mark and appliqué eight 12½-inch and two 11½-inch squares facing this direction.

8. For the remaining eight blocks, refer to the **Reverse Rooster Block Diagram** and flip the

master pattern over before transferring the appliqué design to the background squares. This will give you a mirror image to trace onto the background squares, so that these roosters will face in the opposite direction. Remember to use appliqué pieces R-1 reverse through R-13 reverse when completing these blocks.

9. Mark and appliqué eight 12½-inch and two 11½-inch reverse squares.

Assembling the Quilt Top

1. Referring to the **Quilt Diagram,** place the twenty-five 12½-inch blocks in five vertical rows of five blocks each. Insert a 2 × 12½-inch sashing strip between each block in each row. Sew the blocks and sashing strips together to complete the rows, pressing the seam allowances away from the blocks.

2. Referring to the **Quilt Diagram,** insert a 2 × 66½-inch sashing strip between each of the vertical rows. Sew the rows and sashing strips together, aligning the blocks horizontally before pinning and stitching. Press the seam allowances toward the sashing strips.

3. Referring to the **Quilt Diagram,** sew a 2 × 66½-inch sashing strip to the left and the right edges of the quilt top. Press the seam allowances toward the sashing strips.

4. Referring to the **Quilt Diagram,** sew a 2 × 69½-inch sashing strip to both the top and bottom edges of the quilt top. Press the seam allowances toward the sashing strips.

Appliquéing the Borders

The borders in this quilt have a free-flowing, folk-art quality. At first glance, they seem to be identical, but on closer inspection, you will discover that they are not even symmetrical. So have fun creating borders similar to these, or relax and create some interestingly unique borders of your own design. A few general tips will help you get started:

Each border has a straight stem that springs up from the midpoint and it is crowned with a single appliquéd sunflower. The border vines flow somewhat symmetrically, forming a "mirror image" on either side of this central axis.

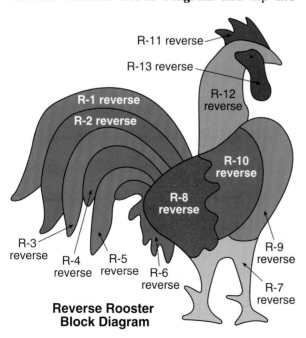

R-11 reverse
R-13 reverse
R-12 reverse
R-1 reverse
R-2 reverse
R-10 reverse
R-8 reverse
R-3 reverse
R-4 reverse
R-5 reverse
R-6 reverse
R-9 reverse
R-7 reverse

Reverse Rooster Block Diagram

Quilt Diagram

Besides this central sunflower, each border contains ten additional sunflowers placed somewhat symmetrically in groups of five on both sides.

The placement of the leaves is much more casual. The top border has 4 large L-1 leaves, 7 medium L-2 leaves, and 8 small L-3 leaves. The right border has 4 large, 1 medium, and 12 small leaves. The bottom border has 4 large, 6 medium, and 9 small leaves. The left border has 4 large, 3 medium, and 10 small leaves. Keeping in mind that these leaves are a mix of both "regular" and "reverse"

leaves, you'll find there is lots of freedom for self-expression in these borders.

1. From the 42-inch square of green fabric, cut bias strips approximately 2¾ inches wide for the vines. Piece, then cut these strips into eight segments, each approximately 48 inches long. Refer to page 158 for more information on making bias strips for stems and vines. Each of these 48-inch-long vines should finish at approximately 1 inch wide.

2. Cut and make 12 more bias segments that finish approximately 1 × 12 inches for the branches.

3. Cut and make 12 more bias segments that finish approximately 1 × 4 inches for the stems.

4. Cut the balance of the square into bias strip approximately ⅛ inch wide. Cut a total of 72 "leaf stem" segments that finish approximately ¼ × 3 inches each. Refer to page 158 for tips on using bias presser bars to make perfect narrow stems.

5. Prepare the S-1 and S-2 sunflower appliqués and all leaf appliqués, according to your preferred method of hand appliqué.

6. Measure the quilt both vertically and horizontally through the center of the quilt top. Trim the 13½ × 72-inch border strips to this measurement.

7. Fold each of the border strips in half lengthwise and crease the midpoints. Referring to the quilt photograph on page 40 and the **Quilt Diagram** on page 45, pin and baste a curving vine in either direction out from this midpoint.

8. Place a branch segment at the midpoint crease and top it with S-1 and S-2 sunflower appliqués. Place another branch diagonally on both sides of the center branch, topping each of these branches with S-1 and S-2 sunflower appliqués. Pin or baste in place.

9. Place four sunflowers along the vine on either side of the central branch. Anchor these sunflowers to the vine with branches as desired. Note that some of the sunflowers are placed right on the vine, without branches. Pin or baste these flowers in place.

10. Scatter the leaves and leaf stems over the balance of the border vine, referring to the quilt photograph and guidelines listed earlier. Pin or baste them in place.

11. Appliqué all border leaves, sunflowers, and vines in place, tucking raw edges of all branches and stems under the appropriate sunflowers and leaves.

12. Appliqué four border panels, labeling them "top," "bottom," "left," and "right," referring to the photograph on page 40, or as desired.

Completing the Rooster Corner Squares

1. Join a 1½ × 11½-inch green sashing strip to the left and the right sides of an 11½-inch Rooster block. Press the seam allowances toward the sashing strips.

2. Sew a 1½ × 13½-inch sashing strip to the top and bottom of the block. Press the seam allowances toward the sashing strips.

3. Make four of these rooster squares for the border corners.

Attaching the Borders to the Quilt Top

1. Mark the midpoints of the "top" and "bottom" appliquéd borders and the top and bottom edges of the quilt top. Matching these midpoints, sew the appliquéd borders to the top and bottom edges of the quilt top. The central branch and sunflower in each border should point toward the outer edge of the quilt. Press the seam allowances toward the outer edges of the quilt.

2. Sew a rooster corner square to each end of the remaining two appliquéd borders, referring to the **Quilt Diagram** on page 45 for placement.

3. Sew a border strip/corner square unit to each side of the quilt, matching midpoints. Press the seams toward the outer edges of the quilt.

Quilting and Finishing

1. Mark quilting designs on the completed quilt top. The quilt shown is quilted in the ditch around each shape in the pieced sunflower, around each sashing strip, and around each appliquéd piece in both blocks and borders. There are veins quilted in each leaf and swirled lines that follow the pattern of the fabric in the center of each sunflower. Additional quilting lines are indicated on pattern D on page 50. The remaining background areas of both blocks and borders are quilted in an overall 1-inch diagonal grid.

2. Divide the backing fabric into three lengths, each measuring 44 × 103½ inches. Remove the selvages and sew the panels together along the long edges. Press the seams open.

3. Layer the quilt back, batting, and quilt top, centering the quilt top so that the seams of the quilt back will be equidistant from both the right and left sides of the quilt top. Baste; then trim the quilt back to approximately 3 inches larger than the quilt top on all sides.

4. Quilt all marked lines, adding additional quilting as desired.

5. From the medium gold binding fabric, make approximately 390 inches of double-fold, straight-grain binding. For instructions on making and attaching binding, see page 164.

6. Sew the binding to the quilt top. Trim excess batting and backing. Using thread to match the binding and an invisible appliqué stitch, hand-sew the folded edge of the binding to the back of the quilt.

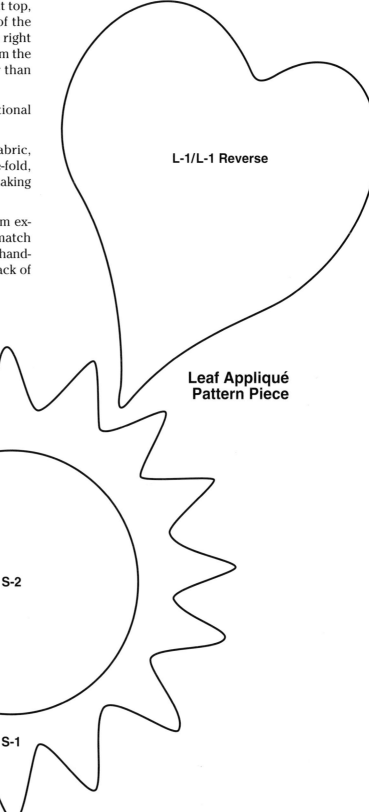

L-1/L-1 Reverse

**Leaf Appliqué
Pattern Piece**

S-2

S-1

Sunflower Appliqué Pattern Pieces

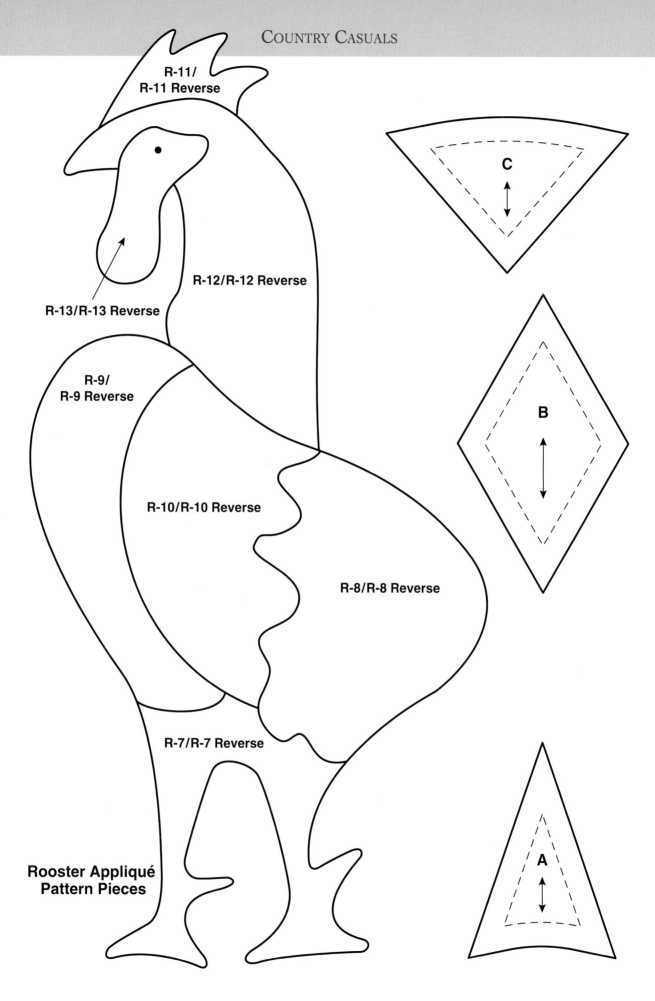

R-11/
R-11 Reverse

R-13/R-13 Reverse

R-12/R-12 Reverse

R-9/
R-9 Reverse

R-10/R-10 Reverse

R-8/R-8 Reverse

R-7/R-7 Reverse

**Rooster Appliqué
Pattern Pieces**

C

B

A

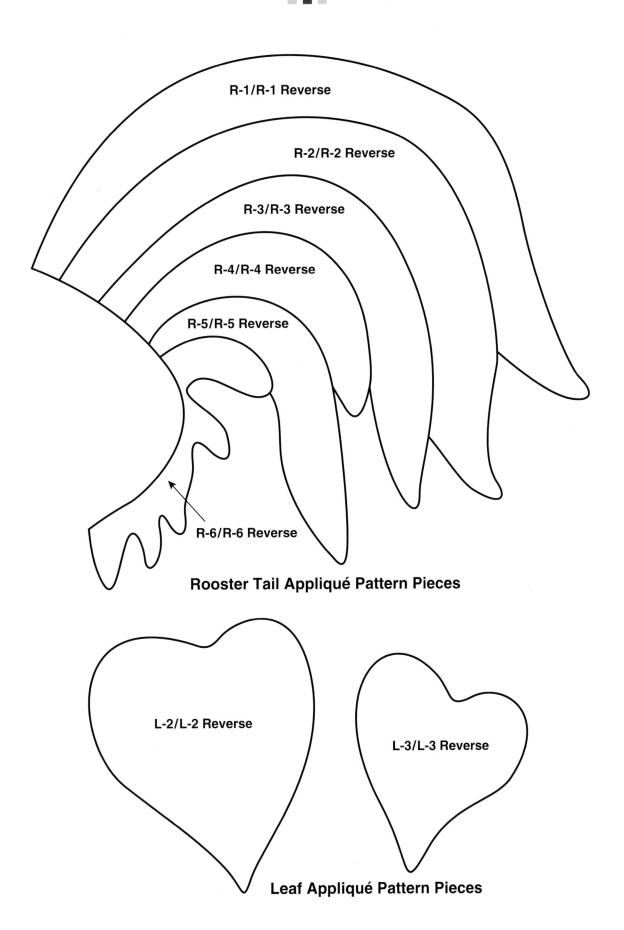

R-1/R-1 Reverse

R-2/R-2 Reverse

R-3/R-3 Reverse

R-4/R-4 Reverse

R-5/R-5 Reverse

R-6/R-6 Reverse

Rooster Tail Appliqué Pattern Pieces

L-2/L-2 Reverse

L-3/L-3 Reverse

Leaf Appliqué Pattern Pieces

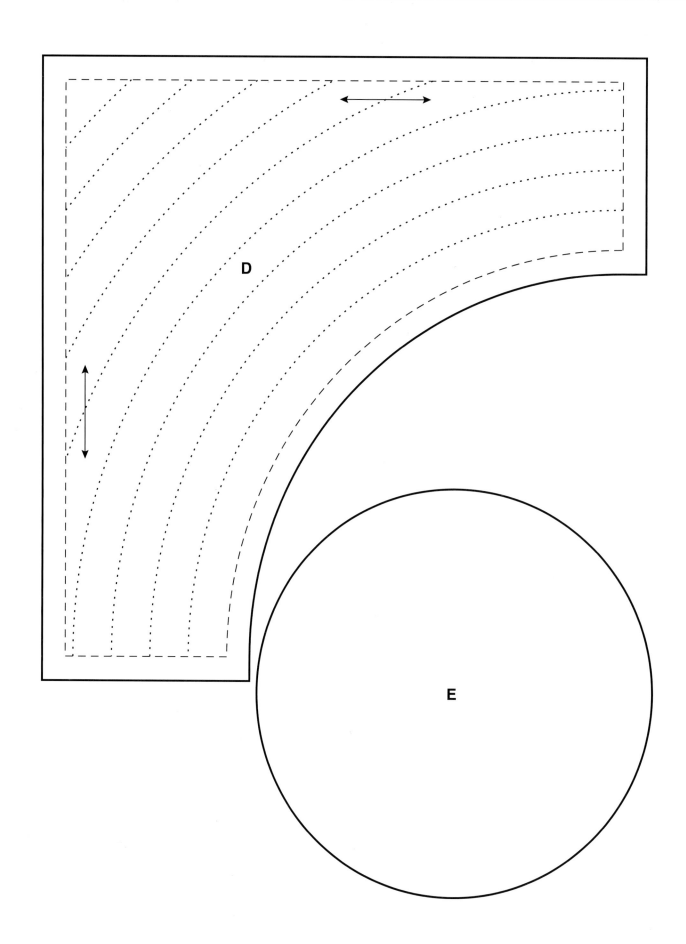

Jim's Scrappy Nine Patch

Quiltmaker: Gloria Greenlee

This wonderful scrap quilt was inspired by an antique quilt discovered in Oklahoma's Heritage Project, which registered pre-1940s quilts. Gloria named the quilt for her husband, who decided while it was still in progress that he wanted to keep it. The quilt offers a great opportunity to use up lots of small fabric scraps in easy Nine-Patch units.

Skill Level: Easy

Size: Finished quilt is 66 × 84 inches
Finished block is 18 inches square

Fabrics and Supplies

- ✓ 3 yards of tan print fabric for triangle squares, pieced border, and binding
- ✓ 2¼ yards of red print fabric for triangle squares and pieced border
- ✓ 1 yard of blue-and-white plaid fabric for middle border
- ✓ ⅓ yard of navy blue print fabric for inner border
- ✓ Approximately 2¼ yards total of assorted medium fabric scraps
- ✓ Approximately 1¾ yards total of assorted light fabric scraps
- ✓ Approximately 1¼ yards total of assorted dark fabric scraps
- ✓ 5 yards of fabric for quilt back
- ✓ Full-size quilt batting (81 × 96 inches)
- ✓ Rotary cutter, ruler, and mat

Cutting

All measurements include ¼-inch seam allowances. The instructions given are for quick-cutting the pieces with a rotary cutter and ruler.

From the tan print fabric, cut:
- 288 triangles: Cut fifteen 3⅞ × 44-inch strips; cut each strip into 3⅞-inch squares. You will need 144 squares. Cut each square in half diagonally to make two triangles.
- Reserve the remaining fabric for binding

From the red print fabric, cut:
- 288 triangles: Cut fifteen 3⅞ × 44-inch strips; cut each strip into 3⅞-inch squares. You will need 144 squares. Cut each square in half diagonally to make two triangles.

From the blue-and-white plaid fabric, cut:
- Eight 3 × 44-inch middle border strips

From the navy blue print fabric, cut:
- Eight 1 × 44-inch inner border strips

From the assorted medium fabric scraps, cut:
- 96 sets of five matching 1½-inch squares each for the dark Nine-Patch units (480 squares total)
- 144 sets of four matching 1½-inch squares each for the light Nine-Patch units (576 squares total)

From the assorted light fabric scraps, cut:
- 144 sets of five matching 1½-inch squares each for the light Nine-Patch units (720 squares total)

From the assorted dark fabric scraps, cut:
- 96 sets of four matching 1½-inch squares each for the dark Nine-Patch units (384 squares total)

Piecing the Nine-Patch Units

The blocks in this quilt are made up of dark Nine-Patch units, light Nine-Patch units, and pieced squares. The dark Nine-Patch units use five medium squares and four dark squares; the light Nine-Patch units use five light squares and four medium squares. Refer to the **Fabric Key** throughout the piecing process.

1. To make a dark Nine-Patch unit you will need one set of five matching medium squares and one set of four matching dark squares. Sew the squares together into three rows, as shown in **Diagram 1**. Press the seams toward the dark squares.

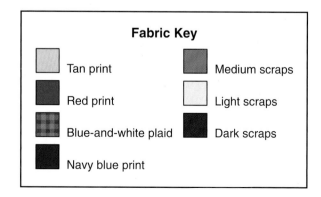

Fabric Key

▢ Tan print	▨ Medium scraps
▧ Red print	▢ Light scraps
▥ Blue-and-white plaid	▨ Dark scraps
▨ Navy blue print	

Diagram 1

2. Join the rows. Press the seams away from the center row. Repeat to make 96 of these units.

3. To make a light Nine-Patch unit you will need one set of five matching light squares and one set of four matching medium squares. Sew the squares together into three rows, as shown in **Diagram 2**. Press the seams toward the medium squares.

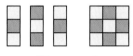

Diagram 2

4. Join the rows. Press the seams away from the center row. Repeat to make 144 of these units.

Making the Pieced-Square Units

1. To make one unit, join a tan print triangle to a red print triangle along the long sides to form a square, as shown in **Diagram 3**. Press the seam toward the red print triangle.

Diagram 3

2. Repeat to make a total of 288 of these pieced-square units. You will need 192 units for the blocks and 96 units for the borders.

Piecing the Blocks

1. Each block is made up of four sections like the one shown in **Diagram 4**. To make each section, lay out two dark Nine Patch units, three light Nine Patch units, and four pieced-square units.

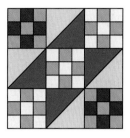

Diagram 4

2. Sew the units together into three rows, as shown in **Diagram 5**. Press the seams toward the pieced-square units. Join the rows, pressing the seams toward the center row. Make 48 of these sections.

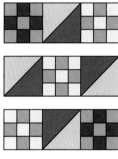

Diagram 5

3. Make 12 large block units by joining sets of four blocks, as shown in the **Unit Diagram**. Joining the blocks together into units helps to cut down on the number of individual blocks that need to be joined.

Unit Diagram

Quilt Diagram

Assembling the Inner Quilt Top

1. Lay out the block units in four horizontal rows with three units in each row, as shown in the **Quilt Diagram**.

2. Sew the blocks together into rows. Press the seams in alternate directions from row to row.

3. Join the rows.

Adding the Borders

1. Piece four inner borders from the 1-inch-wide navy blue border strips. Join one-and-one-half strips each for the top and bottom borders. Join two-and-one-half strips for each of the side borders.

2. Piece four middle borders from the 3-inch-wide blue-and-white plaid border strips. Join one and one-half strips each for the top and bottom borders. Join two and one-half strips for each of the side borders.

3. Sew the navy blue borders to the corresponding length blue-and-white plaid borders to make four border sets. Press the seams away from the navy blue borders.

4. Place the border sets right sides together with the quilt top, matching centers. Sew the border sets to the quilt, mitering the border corner seams. See page 160 for tips on adding mitered borders to a quilt. The quilt should measure 60½ × 78½ inches, including seam allowances.

5. To make the pieced borders for the sides of the quilt top, sew together 26 pieced-square units for each border, positioning the units as shown in the **Quilt Diagram**. Note that the units change direction in the middle of the strips. Press the seams in one direction. Test-fit the borders, and make ad-justments as necessary in the seam allowances if the borders do not fit properly. Sew the borders to the sides of the quilt top, pressing the seams toward the blue-and-white plaid borders.

6. To make the pieced borders for the top and bottom of the quilt top, sew together 22 pieced-square units for each border, again referring to the **Quilt Diagram** for correct positioning. Note that the units change direction in the middle of the strips and at the ends. Press the seams in one direction. Test-fit the borders, and make adjustments as necessary in the seam allowances if the borders do not fit properly. Sew the borders to the top and bottom edges of the quilt top. Press the seams toward the blue-and-white plaid borders.

Quilting and Finishing

1. Mark quilting designs as desired on the finished quilt top. The pattern for the cable design for the border is provided; see the **Border Quilting Design**.

2. Cut the backing fabric into two equal lengths. Trim the selvages, and divide one piece in half lengthwise. Sew a half panel to each side of the full-width panel. Press the seams away from the center panel.

3. Layer the quilt back, batting, and quilt top; baste. Trim the quilt back so it is approximately 3 inches larger than the quilt top on all sides.

4. Quilt all marked designs, and add additional quilting as desired.

5. From the reserved tan print fabric, make approximately 320 inches of double-fold binding. See page 164 for suggested binding widths, instructions, and tips for making and attaching binding.

6. Sew the binding to the quilt top. Trim the excess batting and backing, and hand-sew the folded edge of binding to the back of the quilt.

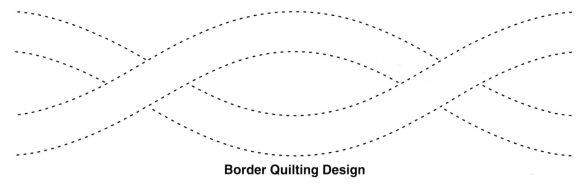

Border Quilting Design

Old Schoolhouse

Quiltmaker: Norma Grasse

Traditional schoolhouse blocks pieced in many different antique black prints are brought to life with red-and-white striped sashing stars. The background fabric is a reproduction of a shirting print that was popular around the turn of the century. Folksy six-pointed star flowers with doughnut holes twinkle between two rows of sawtooth borders. Norma's decision to include a sprinkling of yellow stars among the black and red ones adds the final touch of whimsy.

Skill Level: Intermediate

Size: Finished quilt is 75 inches square
Finished block is 9 inches square

Fabrics and Supplies

- ✓ 5 yards of off-white shirting fabric with black print for borders, houses, sawtooth borders, and sashing strips
- ✓ 1½ yards of black solid fabric for sawtooth borders and binding
- ✓ ⅔ yard *each* of red-and-white stripe fabric and red-and-white print fabric for sashing squares and triangles
- ✓ ½ yard of dark red print fabric for chimneys, border star flowers, and doors
- ✓ ⅓ yard of white-and-red plaid fabric for windows
- ✓ Fat quarters (18 × 22-inch rectangles), or scraps, *each* of 25 black print fabrics for houses and border star flowers
- ✓ Fat quarters (18 × 22-inch rectangles), or scraps, of yellow print for border star flowers
- ✓ 4½ yards of fabric for quilt back
- ✓ Full-size quilt batting (81 × 96 inches)
- ✓ Rotary cutter, ruler, and mat
- ✓ Template plastic

Cutting

All measurements include ¼-inch seam allowances. Measurements for the borders are longer than needed; trim them to the exact length before adding them to the quilt top.

Instructions given are for quick-cutting pieces A through H, X, and Y using a rotary cutter and a ruler. Cut all strips across the fabric unless directed otherwise. Note that for some of the pieces, the quick-cutting method will result in leftover fabric. For the remaining pieces, I through O, V, W, and Z, make templates from the patterns on pages 62–63. Instructions for making and using templates are on page 153. Turn templates over to cut reverse I, O, and W pieces.

You may want to cut just enough pieces to make one block to test your templates, cutting, and seam allowances for accuracy. If your finished block does not measure the size stated above, you can make adjustments before cutting all your fabric.

From the off-white fabric, cut one 74-inch-long piece. From this piece, cut:
- Four 6½ × 74-inch *lengthwise* borders
- 25 *each* of K, M, O, and O reverse pieces for schoolhouse blocks

From the remaining off-white fabric, cut:
- 25 rectangles for the top row of the blocks: Cut seven 1½-inch strips. From these strips cut 25 rectangles, each 1½ × 9½ inches.
- 25 D house rectangles: Cut four 1-inch strips. From these strips cut 25 rectangles, each 1 × 5 inches.
- 344 Y sawtooth triangles: Cut eleven 2⅜-inch strips. From the strips cut 172 squares, each 2⅜ inches square. Cut each square in half diagonally to make two triangles.
- 60 V sashing strips
- One 3½-inch strip for the chimney strip set
- Two 2½-inch strips for the chimney strip set

From the black solid fabric, cut:
- 344 Y sawtooth triangles: Cut eleven 2⅜-inch strips. From the strips cut 172 squares, each 2⅜ inches square. Cut each square in half diagonally to make two triangles.
- Reserve the remaining fabric for binding

From the red-and-white stripe fabric and the red-and-white print fabric, cut a total of:
- 36 X sashing squares: Cut three 2½-inch strips. From the strips cut 36 squares, each 2½ inches square.
- 120 W and 120 W reverse triangles for sashing strips

From the dark red print fabric, cut:
- Two 1½-inch strips for the chimney strip set
- 4 Z border star flowers
- 25 A doors: Cut three 1½-inch strips. Cut the strips into 25 rectangles, each 1½ × 4 inches. Note: One of the doors on the quilt shown was cut from black stripe fabric, rather than from

red print. Feel free to cut additional doors from black fabric.

From the white-and-red plaid fabric, cut:

- 25 H squares for house peak windows: Cut one 1½-inch strip. From this strip cut 25 squares, each 1½ inches square.
- 50 F windows: Cut four 1½-inch strips. From the strips cut 50 rectangles, each 1½ × 3 inches.

From each of the 25 black print fabrics, cut:

- One I, I reverse, J, L, and N piece
- One 1½ × 22-inch strip

  #### From this strip, cut:
  - One 4½-inch C rectangle
  - One 3-inch F rectangle
  - Two 5-inch G rectangles
- Two 2 × 4-inch B rectangles
- Two 1¼ × 3-inch E rectangles

From the remaining black print fabrics, cut:

- 36 Z border star flowers

From the yellow print fabric, cut:

- 4 Z border star flowers

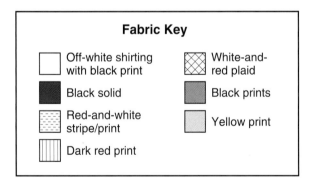

Fabric Key

☐ Off-white shirting with black print	▨ White-and-red plaid
◼ Black solid	▨ Black prints
▨ Red-and-white stripe/print	☐ Yellow print
▥ Dark red print	

Piecing the Blocks

Each block is assembled in four rows: chimney (row 3), roof (row 2), and bottom of the house (row 1). Row 4 is simply a strip of background fabric added to the top of the block. See **Block Diagram.**

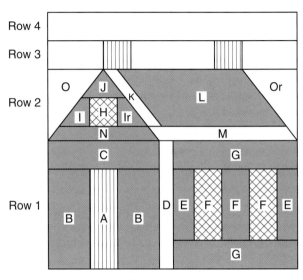

Block Diagram

Making the Chimney Sections

1. Referring to the **Fabric Key** and **Diagram 1,** sew a 1½-inch dark red print strip to the long sides of a 3½-inch off-white strip. Sew a 2½-inch off-white strip to the remaining long side of each red strip. Press the seam allowances toward the red strips.

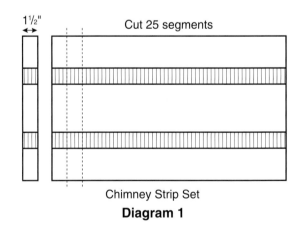

Chimney Strip Set
Diagram 1

2. Cut the chimney strip set into 25 segments, each 1½ inches wide.

Assembling the Schoolhouse Blocks

Refer to the **Block Diagram** to piece 25 Schoolhouse blocks. Make sure that all black pieces for a single block are from the same black print fabric.

1. To make the house front, sew a black print B rectangle to the long sides of a dark red A door piece. Press seam allowances toward the B pieces. Sew a black print C rectangle to the top edge of the door unit to complete the house front. See **Diagram 2.**

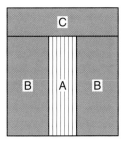

House Front
Diagram 2

2. To make the house side, sew a white-and-red plaid F window rectangle to each long edge of a black print F rectangle. Add a black print E rectangle to the remaining long edge of the plaid rectangles. See **Diagram 3.** Press seam allowances away from the F windows. Sew a black print G rectangle to the top and bottom edges of the house side to complete the house side unit.

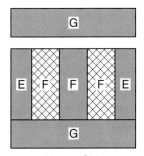

House Side
Diagram 3

3. To complete Row 1 of the block, sew an off-white D rectangle to the right side of the house front unit. Sew the house side unit to the opposite side of the D rectangle. Press the seam allowances away from the D rectangle. See **Diagram 4.**

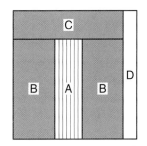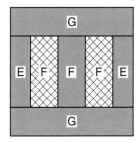

Row 1
Diagram 4

4. To make the house peak, sew black print I and I reverse pieces to opposite sides of a white-and-red plaid H window square. Press seam allowances away from the window. Sew a black print J triangle to the top edge of the H/I unit and a black print N piece to the bottom edge. Press seam allowances away from the H/I unit. See **Diagram 5.** Sew an off-white O triangle to the left side of the house peak. Press the seam allowances toward the O piece.

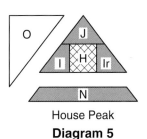

House Peak
Diagram 5

5. To complete the roof section, sew an off-white K piece to the left slanted edge of a black print L roof piece, as in **Diagram 6.** Press the seam allowance toward the roof. Sew an off-white M piece to the lower edge of the K/L unit. Press seam allowances toward M. Add an off-white O reverse triangle to the right slanted edge of the L roof piece. Press seam allowances toward O reverse.

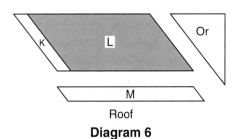

Roof
Diagram 6

6. Join the house peak and roof sections by sewing the long edge of piece K to the diagonal edge of the house peak unit to make Row 2.

7. Join Rows 1 and 2, being careful to match the roof peak seam intersections with those of the house front. See the **Block Diagram.**

8. Sew a chimney segment to the top edge of the house. Press seam allowances toward the chimney segment.

9. Sew a 1½ × 9½-inch off-white piece to the top edge of the chimney segment to complete the block. Your block should measure 9½ inches square, including seam allowances.

10. Repeat to make a total of 25 Schoolhouse blocks, each using a different black print fabric.

Assembling the Quilt Top

1. To piece one sashing strip, sew a red-and-white stripe or print W and W reverse triangle to each slanted end of an off-white V sashing strip as

shown in **Diagram 7.** Press the seam allowances toward the W pieces. Make 60 sashing strips.

Make 60

Sashing Strip
Diagram 7

2. Referring to the **Quilt Assembly Diagram,** sew the Schoolhouse blocks together in five horizontal rows with five blocks and six sashing strips in each row. Press seam allowances toward the blocks.

3. Make six horizontal sashing rows with six red-and-white stripe or print X sashing squares and five sashing strips in each row. Press the seam allowances toward the sashing squares.

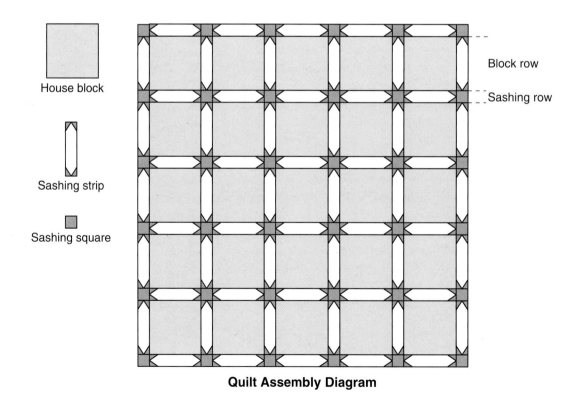

House block

Sashing strip

Sashing square

Block row

Sashing row

Quilt Assembly Diagram

4. Join the rows, beginning with a sashing row and alternating types of rows. Press the seam allowances to one side.

Adding the Borders

1. Sew an off-white Y triangle to a black solid Y triangle along their long diagonal edges to form a triangle-square, as shown in **Diagram 8.** Press the seam allowance toward the black triangle. Repeat to make a total of 344 black and off-white triangle-squares.

Triangle-Square
Diagram 8

2. Referring to the photo on page 56 for the direction of the slant of triangle-square seams, make sawtooth borders. Join 37 triangle-square units for the inner top and bottom borders. Join 39 triangle-square units for the inner side borders. Join 47 triangle-square units for the outer top and bottom borders, and 49 triangle-square units for the outer side borders. Press seam allowances to one side.

3. Sew the 37-unit sawtooth borders to the top and bottom edges of the quilt top. Sew the 39-unit sawtooth borders to the sides of the quilt top. Press seam allowances toward the quilt top.

4. Trim two off-white border strips to 60½ inches. This should be the width of your quilt. Sew the off-white borders to the top and bottom edges of the quilt, easing either the quilt or the borders to fit if necessary. Press seam allowances toward the off-white borders.

5. Trim two off-white border strips to 72½ inches. Sew the borders to the sides of the quilt top, easing to fit if necessary. Press seam allowances toward the off-white borders.

6. Sew the 47-unit sawtooth borders to the top and bottom of the quilt. Sew the 49-unit sawtooth borders to the sides of the quilt top. Press seam allowances toward the off-white borders.

EASIER APPLIQUÉ

It is easier to appliqué if you do not cut out the center circle until after you have appliquéd the star flower to your border. When cutting out the circle, be sure to add a scant ¼-inch seam allowance to the inside edge of the circle.

7. Prepare the Z star flowers for appliqué. Instructions for appliqué are on page 157. Pin a star flower at each corner of the off-white border. Then pin ten star flowers along each border evenly spaced between the corner star flowers. Appliqué the star flowers in place.

Quilting and Finishing

1. Mark desired quilting designs. The border is quilted with a diagonal grid of 1-inch squares, and the houses are outline quilted and filled in with parallel line quilting.

2. To piece the quilt back, cut the backing fabric into two 2¼-yard pieces. Cut one piece in half lengthwise. Sew a half panel to each long side of the full panel. Press the seam allowances toward the outer panels.

3. Layer the quilt back, batting, and quilt top; baste. Trim the quilt back and batting so they are approximately 3 inches larger than the quilt top on all sides.

4. Quilt all marked designs, and add additional quilting as desired.

5. Make approximately 320 inches of French-fold binding from the black solid fabric. See page 164 for instructions on making and attaching binding.

6. Sew the binding to the quilt. Trim the excess batting and backing, and hand-sew the folded edge of the binding to the wrong side of the quilt. Refer to page 165 for instructions on making and attaching a hanging sleeve.

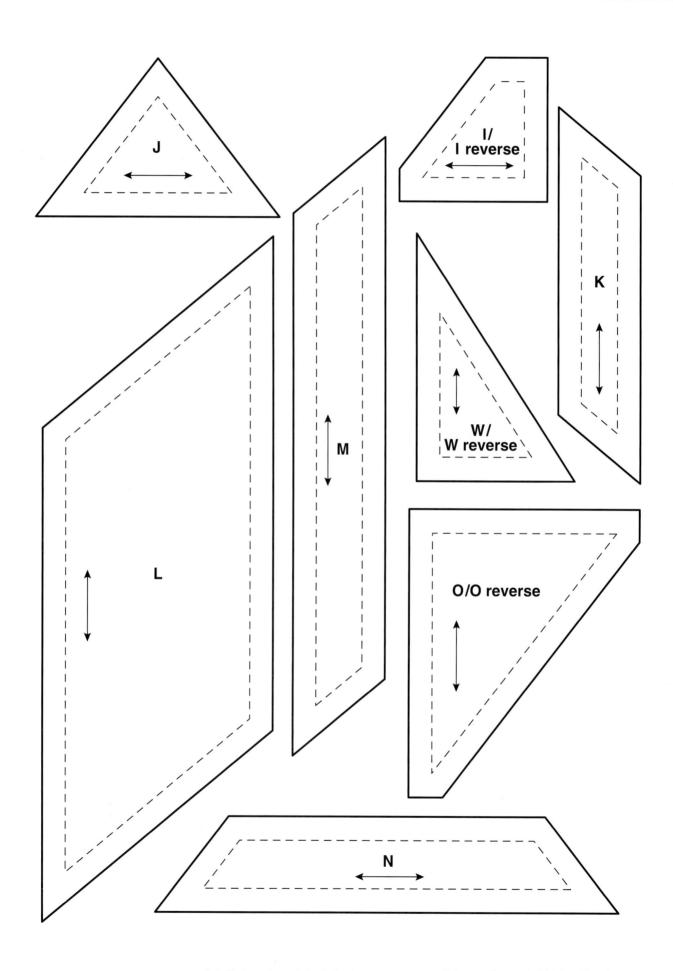

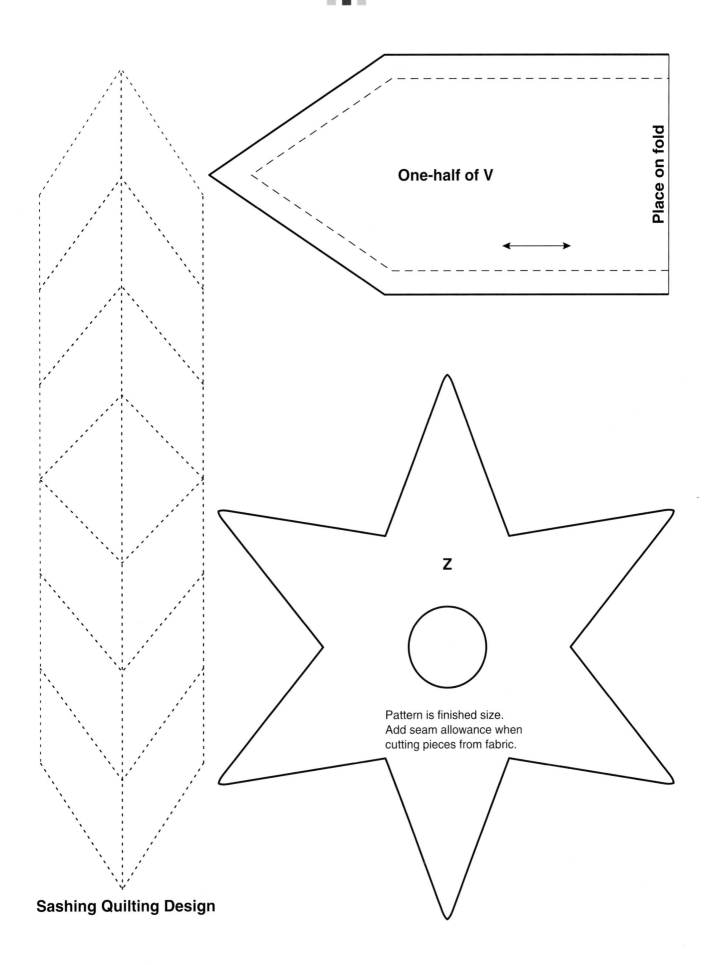

One-half of V

Place on fold

Z

Pattern is finished size.
Add seam allowance when
cutting pieces from fabric.

Sashing Quilting Design

Brick Wall

Quiltmaker: Tina M. Gravatt

The large antique quilt from around the turn of the century provided inspiration for the brand-new miniature. The old one is a scrap quilt, made from a variety of similar medium blue or "indigo" prints, combined with "shirtings," white fabrics with small black figures. The new quilt uses current reproduction patterns. Rotary cutting and strip piecing make either project quick and easy to sew. Both are tied rather than quilted.

Skill Level: Easy

Size: Finished large quilt is 71½ × 87½ inches

Finished bricks are 2¾ × 5 inches
Finished miniature quilt is 18 × 25⅜ inches
Finished bricks are 1 × 1¾ inches

Fabrics and Supplies for Large Quilt

- ✓ ½ yard *each* of seven medium blue print fabrics for patchwork
- ✓ ½ yard *each* of seven white-and-black print fabrics for patchwork
- ✓ 5½ yards of fabric for quilt back
- ✓ ¾ yard of fabric for binding
- ✓ Full-size quilt batting (81 × 96 inches)
- ✓ Rotary cutter, ruler, and mat
- ✓ Cotton or synthetic yarn for tying
- ✓ Darning needle

Cutting

All measurements include ¼-inch seam allowances. Instructions given are for quick-cutting the strips for strip piecing.

From each of the blue print fabrics, cut:
- Three 5½ × 44-inch strips

From each of the white-and-black print fabrics, cut:
- Three 5½ × 44-inch strips

Making the Quilt

1. Sew strips together as shown in **Diagram 1**, using the one blue print and one white-and-black print strip per set. Make a total of 21 strip sets. Press seams toward the blue fabric strips.

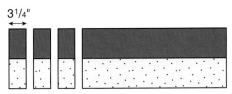

3¼"

Diagram 1

2. Cut 3¼-inch-wide segments from the strip sets, as shown in the diagram. You should be able to cut 12 or 13 segments from each strip set. You will need a total of 234 segments.

3. Join the cut segments end to end to make 26 long strips of alternating blue and white rectangles, with 9 segments per strip. In the miniature quilt, each long strip is made up of only one blue fabric. In the antique, however, the use of blue fabrics is more random. Decide on the effect you want to create, and piece the strips and segments accordingly.

4. Referring to the **Quilt Diagram** and the photo on page 64, lay out the 26 strips, offsetting the matching color brick rectangles by one-half rectangle as shown. (The heavy lines on the quilt diagram show the layout of the miniature quilt.) Turn strips end for end as needed to position blue or white segments properly. The top and bottom edges of the quilt will be uneven.

5. Before joining the long strips, make positioning marks on the wrong side as described in

Quilt Diagram

"Making Positioning Marks for Joining Strips." This ensures that the rectangles will be offset evenly. Join the rows, aligning the positioning marks with the seams. Press the seams in one direction.

6. Trim the uneven top and bottom edges of the quilt.

Finishing

1. Cut the backing fabric into two equal 99-inch lengths and trim the selvages. Divide one piece in half lengthwise. Sew a half panel to each side of the full panel. Press seams away from the center panel.

2. Layer the backing, batting, and quilt top. Use a darning needle and cotton yarn to make ties at corners of seams as desired. See "How to Tie a Comforter" for complete directions.

3. From the binding fabric, make approximately 350 inches of double-fold binding. See page 164 for suggested binding widths and instructions on making and attaching binding.

4. Sew the binding to the quilt top. Trim the excess batting and backing, and hand-sew the folded edge of the binding to the back side of the quilt.

Fabrics and Supplies for Miniature Quilt

- ✓ Six 2¼ × 44-inch medium blue print fabric strips
- ✓ Six 2¼ × 44-inch white-and-black print fabric strips
- ✓ 1 yard of fabric for quilt back and binding
- ✓ Quilt batting, larger than 18 × 25⅜ inches
- ✓ Rotary cutter, ruler, and mat
- ✓ Cotton or synthetic yarn for tying
- ✓ Darning needle

Making the Quilt

1. Sew strips together as shown in **Diagram 2**, using one blue and one white-and-black strip per set. Make a total of 6 strip sets. Press the seams toward the blue fabric strip.

MAKING POSITIONING MARKS FOR JOINING STRIPS

The long strips of rectangular "bricks" are offset by one-half brick from row to row. Before joining rows, make positioning indicators on the wrong side of the fabric at the middle of the white-and-black bricks, as shown in the diagram.

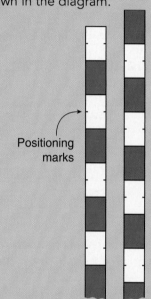

Positioning marks

Make indicators either by measuring and making pencil marks or by folding bricks and making crease marks. If measuring, for the large quilt, mark the bricks 2½ inches away from seams; for the miniature, mark ⅞ inch from seams. Pin rows together before joining them, aligning the marks with the seams to stagger the bricks exactly one-half brick from row to row.

2. Cut 1½-inch-wide segments from the strip sets, as shown in the diagram. You will need 24 segments from each strip set, for a total of 144 segments.

1½"

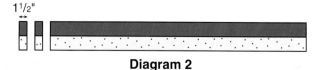

Diagram 2

3. Join the cut segments end to end to make 18 long strips of alternating blue and white rectangles, with 8 segments per strip. In the miniature quilt, only one color brick is used in each strip, and the three same-color strips are placed together in the layout.

4. Referring to the **Quilt Diagram** and the photo on page 64, lay out the 18 strips, offsetting the matching color brick rectangles by one-half rectangle as shown. The heavy lines on the diagram show the layout for the miniature quilt. Turn strips end for end as needed to position blue or white segments properly. The top and bottom edges of the quilt will be uneven.

5. Before joining the long strips, make positioning marks on the wrong side as described in "Making Positioning Marks for Joining Strips." This ensures that the segments will be offset evenly. Join the rows, aligning the offset marks with seams. Press the seams in one direction.

6. Trim the uneven top and bottom edges of the quilt.

Finishing

1. Cut a 22 × 30-inch piece of backing fabric.

2. Layer the backing, batting, and quilt top. Use a darning needle and yarn to make ties at corners of seams as desired. See "How to Tie a Comforter" below for complete directions.

3. From the binding fabric, make approximately 100 inches of double-fold binding. See page 164 for suggested binding widths and instructions on making and attaching binding.

4. Sew the binding to the quilt top. Trim the excess batting and backing fabric, and hand-sew the folded edge of the binding to the back of the quilt.

HOW TO TIE A COMFORTER

For a tied comforter, choose a stable, synthetic batting designed for tying. Many cotton batts must be quilted at close intervals or the filler will wad up when laundered. For tied comforters, you can use a high-loft batt that provides lots of warmth. Follow the steps below to make sturdy ties.

1. Thread a darning needle with a long length of yarn; don't knot the end. Experiment to see what length yarn works best for you.

2. Make a small stitch at a seam intersection for a tie. Be sure the stitch goes through all layers.

3. Pull up the yarn, leaving a 3- to 4-inch-long tail. Do not cut the yarn at this point (after you use the entire length of yarn you will cut between stitches and then make a knot).

4. Move to the next tie position and make another stitch. Leave a long, loose length of yarn between each stitch you take at the seam intersections. Continue to make small stitches at seam intersections, rethreading the needle as necessary.

5. Clip the middle of the yarn between seam intersection stitches.

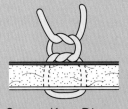

6. Tie a square knot. Begin by holding the two ends of the yarn in your right and left hands. Wrap the right yarn tail around the left; tighten the half-knot. Complete the knot by wrapping the left tail around the right, as shown in the **Square Knot Diagram**. Tighten the knot.

Square Knot Diagram

7. Gather the yarn tails into one hand and clip to the desired length.

Note: If you want a fuller-looking, bulky knot, cut one or two 6-inch-long pieces of yarn and lay them atop the small stitch at each seam intersection after the first half of the knot is tied. See the **Bulky Knot Diagram**. Treat the original yarn ends and the added ends as one when completing the square knot, as shown in the diagram.

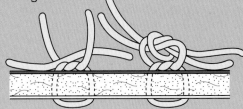

Bulky Knot Diagram

Patchwork Pillows

Quiltmaker: Cyndi Hershey

Traditional patchwork patterns and warm earthtone fabrics combine in these pretty toss pillows. Cyndi's unusual edge finishes add a special touch. These pillows offer a great opportunity to experiment with scraps on a small scale before plunging into a large project. You can build your scrap confidence and make a quick gift at the same time!

Skill Level: Intermediate

▸ Double Nine-Patch Pillow

Size: Finished Double Nine-Patch Pillow is approximately 20 inches square, including ruffle (14¾ inches without ruffle)

Fabrics and Supplies for the Double Nine-Patch Pillow with Ruffle

✓ ½ yard of cream print fabric for corner setting triangles, framing strips, and pillow back

✓ ¼ yard *each* of four dark print fabrics for patchwork and ruffle

✓ One scrap (approximately 5 inches square) or an additional dark print fabric for patchwork

✓ Scraps (approximately 5 inches square) of five light print fabrics for patchwork

✓ Scraps (approximately 4 inches square) of four medium print fabrics for patchwork

✓ One 18-inch square of quilt batting

✓ One 18-inch square of muslin for lining

✓ Polyester fiberfill

✓ Rotary cutter, ruler, and mat

Cutting

All measurements include seam allowances; sew seam using ¼-inch seams unless directed otherwise. Instructions are given for quick-cutting the pieces with a rotary cutter and ruler.

From the cream print fabric, cut:
• One 16-inch-square pillow back

• Two 7½-inch squares. Cut each square in half diagonally to make two triangles, for a total of four corner setting triangles.

• Four 1¾ × 16-inch framing strips

From each of the four dark print fabrics, cut:
• Two 6 × 18-inch rectangles for ruffle

• Five 1½-inch A squares for nine-patch units

From the dark print scrap, cut:
• Five 1½-inch A squares for nine-patch units

From each of the five light print scrap fabrics, cut:
• Four 1½-inch A squares for nine-patch units

From each of the four medium print scrap fabrics, cut:
• One 3½-inch B square

Piecing the Pillow Top

1. Begin by making the five small Nine-Patch blocks. For each small block, lay out five matching dark A squares and four matching light A squares.

2. Referring to the **Fabric Key** and **Diagram 1** on page 70, join the nine squares into three rows of three squares per row. Press the seams toward the dark squares. Join the rows, pressing the seams in one direction. Make a total of five blocks.

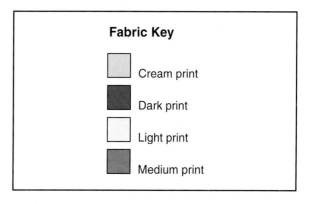

Fabric Key

☐ Cream print

■ Dark print

☐ Light print

■ Medium print

Diagram 1

3. Lay out the five pieced blocks with the four B squares. Join the blocks and squares to make three rows, as shown in **Diagram 2**. Press the seams toward the B squares. Join the rows.

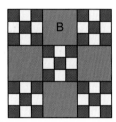

Diagram 2

4. Sew a cream print corner setting triangle to two opposite sides of the completed block. Press the seams toward the triangles. Sew the remaining two cream triangles to the remaining sides of the block; press the seams toward the triangles.

5. Trim two of the 1¾-inch-wide framing strips to the size of the block. Sew the strips to two opposite sides of the squared-off block. Press the seams toward the framing strips.

6. Measure the sides of the block including the framing strips. Trim the two remaining 1¾-inch-wide framing strips to this measurement. Sew them to the remaining two sides of the block to complete the pillow top, as shown in the **Nine-Patch Pillow Diagram**.

Nine-Patch Pillow Diagram

Quilting the Pillow Top

1. Layer the completed pillow top, the square of batting, and the muslin lining square; baste the layers together.

2. Quilt as desired. The pillow shown was machine quilted with parallel lines approximately ¾ inch apart.

Making the Ruffle and Assembling the Pillow

1. Sew the eight 6 × 18-inch dark print rectangles together end to end, alternating the prints. You will have a long strip 6 inches wide by approximately 140 inches long. Press the seams open.

2. Join the two ends of the strip to make a big loop. Press the strip in half lengthwise, wrong sides together.

3. Machine stitch two lines of large gathering stitches ¼ inch and ⅛ inch in from the raw edge of the ruffle loop.

4. Working with the quilted pillow top right side up, arrange the ruffle loop so that two pieced sections of it will fall on each side of the pillow top. Line up and pin a ruffle seam at the center of each side of the pillow top; line up and pin the remaining ruffle seams close to the corners of the pillow top.

5. Draw up the gathering threads on the ruffle, and pin in to the pillow top, matching raw edges. Space the gathers evenly along the pillow edge, allowing extra fullness at the corners.

6. Machine baste the gathered ruffle to the pillow top with a ¼-inch seam. Pin the folded edge of the ruffle to the pillow top in several places so it won't get caught in the seam when you sew the back on. Trim away excess batting and lining.

7. Pin the pillow top to the back, right sides together. The ruffle will be hidden inside the layers. Sewing from the pillow top side rather than from the pillow back side, machine stitch around the pillow, taking a ⅜-inch seam allowance. Leave a 7½-inch opening along one side for turning and stuffing. Trim the excess backing fabric.

8. Turn the pillow right side out through the opening, and stuff it firmly with polyester filling. Hand stitch the opening closed.

▸ Straight Furrows Pillow

Size: Finished Straight Furrows Pillow is 12 × 16 inches

Fabrics and Supplies for the Straight Furrows Pillow

- ✓ ½ yard of medium print fabric for border and pillow back

- ✓ Scraps (approximately 5 inches square) of 12 dark print fabrics for patchwork*

- ✓ Scraps (approximately 3 inches square) of 12 light print fabrics for patchwork*

- ✓ One 20 × 16-inch piece of muslin for lining

- ✓ One 20 × 16-inch piece of quilt batting

- ✓ Polyester fiberfill

- ✓ Rotary cutter, ruler, and mat

* Choose fabrics that have lots of contrast so the Straight Furrows pattern shows up nicely; see the **Straight Furrows Pillow Diagram** for inspiration.

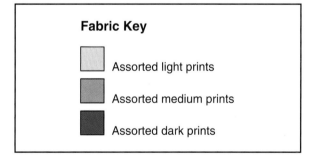

Fabric Key

▢ Assorted light prints

▨ Assorted medium prints

▩ Assorted dark prints

Cutting

All measurements include ¼-inch seam allowances. The instructions given are for quick-cutting the pieces with a rotary cutter and ruler.

From the medium print fabric, cut:
- One 12½ × 16½-inch pillow back

- Two 1½ × 14½-inch border strips
- Two 1½ × 8½-inch border strips

From each of the dark print scraps, cut:
- One 2⅞-inch square, for a total of twelve squares

- Two 1½ × 2½-inch rectangles for pieced border. Cut two additional rectangles from your favorite dark scraps for a total of fourteen pieces.

From the light print scrap fabrics, cut:
- One 2⅞-inch square from each fabric for a total of twelve light squares

Piecing the Pillow Top

1. Referring to **Diagram 1**, draw a diagonal line from one corner to another on the reverse side of each light square.

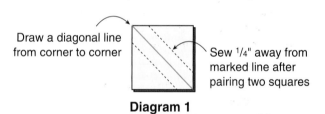

Draw a diagonal line from corner to corner

Sew ¹/₄" away from marked line after pairing two squares

Diagram 1

2. Pair a 2⅞-inch light square with a dark square of the same size, right sides together and edges matched.

3. Sew each pair together with two seams as shown in **Diagram 1**, each ¼ inch from the marked line. If you don't have a ¼-inch presser foot, draw the seam lines, too, before beginning. Repeat for all 2⅞-inch squares.

4. Use scissors or rotary cutting equipment to cut through both layers of squares on the marked diagonal line.

5. *Before* you open up the unit, press a medium hot iron onto each sewn unit at the seam line, "setting" the seam as it was sewn. You'll need to take great care not to distort or stretch the units as you press the seams: Open a unit by flipping up the dark triangle, making sure the seam allowance is towards the dark fabric, as shown in **Diagram 2**. Carefully move the iron into the diagonal seam line that separates the dark half from the light half, pressing by lifting the iron with an up and down motion and not by sliding the iron along the seamline. Open up and press all units, as shown in the diagram. Trim away the seam allowance nubs at two corners.

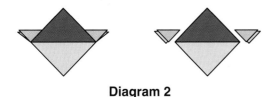

Diagram 2

6. Referring to the **Straight Furrows Pillow Diagram**, lay out the pieced-squares in six vertical rows of four units per row. Position the fabrics so that the diagonal "straight furrow" strips are formed as shown in the diagram.

7. Sew the units together into rows. Press the seams in opposite directions from row to row. Join the rows.

8. Sew the 1½ × 8½-inch medium print fabric border strips to the two short sides of the pieced rectangle. Press the seams toward the border strips. Sew the 1½ × 14½-inch border strips to the two long sides of the rectangle; press the seams toward the strips.

9. Join the dark fabric rectangles in random order to make four pieced border strips. Make two strips with five rectangles each and two strips with eight rectangles each.

10. Sew the two shorter pieced borders to the two short sides of the pillow top; press the seams toward the borders. Sew the two longer pieced borders to the two long sides of the pillow top; press the seams toward the borders.

Quilting and Finishing the Pillow

1. Layer the completed pillow top, batting, and muslin lining; baste the layers together.

2. Quilt as desired. The pillow shown was machine quilted ¼ inch away from the diagonal seams on the light triangle strips, as well as in the ditch along the border seams. After quilting, trim excess batting and lining even with the pillow top.

3. Pin the pillow top to the back, right sides together. Using a ¼-inch seam allowance, machine stitch around the pillow, leaving a 7½-inch opening along one side for turning and stuffing.

4. Turn the pillow right side out through the opening, and stuff it firmly with polyester filling. Hand-sew the opening closed.

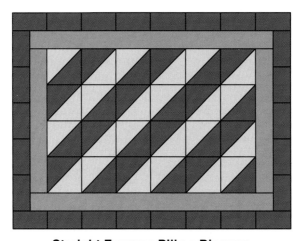

Straight Furrows Pillow Diagram

► Morning Star Pillow

Size: Finished Morning Star Pillow is 14 inches square

Fabrics and Supplies for the Morning Star Pillow

- ✓ ⅛ yard or scraps of dark green fabric for patchwork
- ✓ ⅛ yard or scraps of off-white print fabric for patchwork
- ✓ ⅛ yard or scraps of rust print fabric for patchwork and border strips
- ✓ Two scraps (approximately 6½ inches square) of gold print fabric for setting triangles
- ✓ Two scraps (approximately 4½ inches square) of black print fabric for corner triangles
- ✓ ⅝ yard of assorted medium and dark fabrics strips for covered cording. Strips can vary in length, but must be at least 1¾ inches tall.
- ✓ One 18-inch square of muslin for lining
- ✓ One 14½-inch square of fabric for pillow back
- ✓ One 18-inch square of quilt batting
- ✓ 1⅔ yards of ⅜-inch-diameter cable cord
- ✓ Polyester fiberfill
- ✓ Rotary cutter, ruler with 45-degree angle line, and mat

Cutting

All measurements include seam allowances; sew ¼-inch seams unless directed otherwise. Patchwork is constructed using quick cutting and piecing techniques.

From the dark green fabric, cut:
- One 1¾ × 44-inch strip

From the off-white print fabric, cut:
- Two 1¾ × 44-inch strips for D diamond units

From the rust print fabric, cut:
- One 1¾ × 44-inch strip for D diamond units
- Four 1½ × 16-inch border strips

From the gold print fabric, cut:
- Two 6¼-inch squares. Cut each square both ways diagonally to make four E triangles.

From the black print fabric, cut:
- Two 4⅜-inch squares. Cut each square in half diagonally to make two E triangles.

From the assorted medium and dark strips, cut:
- Several 1¾-inch-wide strips. Use your rotary ruler to cut a 45-degree angle at the left edge of a strip as shown in **Diagram 1A**. Align the ruler's 1¾-inch line with the angled left edge and a 45-degree marked line with the bottom edge of the strip as shown in **Diagram 1B**. Cut segment. Repeat to make a total of 35 diamonds.

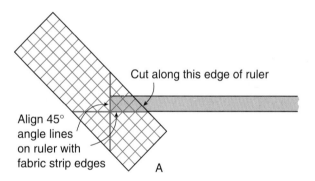

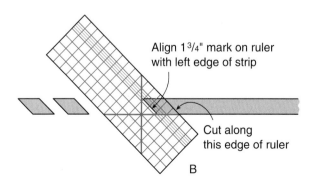

Diagram 1

Quick-Piecing the Diamonds for the Star

1. Referring to the **Fabric Key** and **Diagram 2**, make two strip sets using the green, off-white, and rust strips. Press the seams toward the darker fabrics.

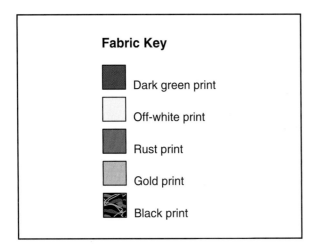

Fabric Key

■ Dark green print

□ Off-white print

■ Rust print

■ Gold print

▨ Black print

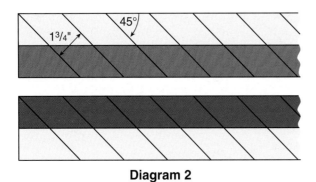

1¾"   45°

Diagram 2

2. Using the 45-degree angle line on your ruler, cut eight 1¾-inch-wide diamond units from each strip set, as shown in **Diagram 2**.

3. Lay out the diamond units in pairs, as shown in **Diagram 3**. Join the units into sections. You will have eight large diamond sections.

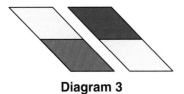

Diagram 3

Piecing the Star

1. Lay out the large diamond sections and the E triangles, as shown in the **Morning Star Pillow Diagram**. Place the green diamonds toward the center.

E

D

Morning Star Pillow Diagram

2. Referring to **Diagram 4**, join the large diamond sections in pairs. When joining the diamond sections, begin stitching at the center of the star. Stop stitching exactly ¼ inch from the

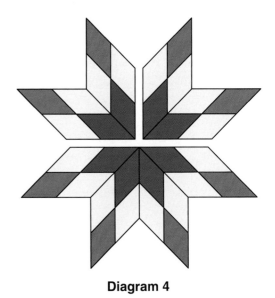

Diagram 4

outside raw edge; do not stitch into the seam allowance on the outside edge of the star.

3. Join the pairs as shown to form two half stars. Stop stitching ¼ inch from the outer edge so that the seams are free at the corners to set in squares and triangles. In the same manner, join the two halves of the star to complete it.

4. Set four of the gold E triangles into alternate openings around the star. See page 155 for tips on setting-in pieces.

5. Join the black E print triangles and the remaining gold triangles to form four corner squares. Set a square into each corner, placing the black print triangle to the outside.

Adding the Borders

1. Measure the block, and trim two of the 1½-inch-wide rust print border strips to this size (approximately 12½ inches). Sew the borders to two opposite sides of the completed block. Press the seams toward the borders.

2. Measure the block including the side borders. Trim the two remaining rust strips to this size (approximately 14½ inches), and sew them to the block. Press the seams toward the borders.

Quilting and Finishing the Pillow

1. Mark quilting designs. Layer the completed pillow top, batting, and muslin lining; baste the layers together.

2. Quilt as desired. The pillow shown was machine quilted in the ditch and with parallel lines in the gold triangles. When quilting is complete, trim the excess batting and lining even with the pillow top.

3. Use the 35 diamonds cut from scraps to make the covered cording for the edge. Join the diamonds in random order to make a long strip. Press the seam allowances in one direction.

4. With the wrong side next to the cording, wrap the pieced strip around the cording and baste the raw edges together close to the cording, encasing the cording within the strip.

5. Baste the cording to the front of the pillow top, aligning the raw edge of the encased cording with the raw edge of the pillow top.

6. Pin the pillow top to the back, with right sides facing. Using a ¼-inch seam allowance, machine stitch around the pillow, leaving a 7½-inch opening on one side for turning and stuffing.

7. Turn the pillow to the right side through the opening. Stuff the pillow firmly with polyester filling. Hand-sew the opening closed.

Plaid Pleasures

Country Wedding Ring
Plaid Folk Hearts
Stargazing with Roberta
Escargot in Plaid
Plaid Spools

■

Country Wedding Ring

Quiltmaker: Susan Stein

Plaids and stripes combine beautifully in this dramatic wall quilt. The richness of Susan's quilt is enhanced by the combination of a deep dark background stripe with Wedding Rings in much lighter color values. Eight different plaids form the Wedding Rings, and each ring is separated by an eye-catching hint of the same black and beige plaid she chose for the binding.

Skill Level: Intermediate

Size: Finished quilt is 42 × 52 inches

Fabrics and Supplies

- ✓ 1½ yards of medium red striped fabric for the background in the rings
- ✓ 1½ yards of red print for the quilt background
- ✓ ¼ yard *each* of four different light plaid fabrics for the rings
- ✓ ¼ yard *each* of two different medium plaid fabrics for the rings
- ✓ ¼ yard *each* of two different dark plaid fabrics for the rings
- ✓ ½ yard of a black/beige plaid fabric for the rings and binding
- ✓ 1⅝ yards of fabric for the quilt back
- ✓ Crib-size batting (4 × 60 inches)
- ✓ Template material

Cutting

Pattern pieces A through E are provided on page 82. The patterns include ¼-inch seam allowances. As you decide which plaid or striped fabric to cut for each of the pieces, refer to the quilt photograph for fabric placement.

From the medium red striped fabric, cut:
- 16 B pieces on the lengthwise grain of the fabric
- 15 B pieces on the crosswise grain of the fabric
- 12 A pieces

From light plaid fabrics, cut:
- A *total* of 124 C pieces: 62 from one plaid fabric and 62 from another plaid fabric
- 62 D pieces

From medium plaid fabrics, cut:
- 62 D reverse pieces
- 62 C pieces
- 30 E pieces

From dark plaid fabrics, cut:
- 62 C pieces

From the black/beige plaid fabric, cut:
- 32 E pieces

Piecing the Wedding Rings

1. Referring to **Diagram 1,** sew together a medium plaid C piece, a light plaid C, a dark plaid C, and a light plaid C, as shown. Add a medium D reverse piece to one end and a light D piece to the other end, as shown. Press the seam allowances to one side. Make a total of 62 of these pieced arcs.

2. Referring to **Diagram 2,** sew a black/beige plaid E piece to each end of 16 of these pieced arcs, as shown. Sew a medium plaid E piece to each end of 15 of the pieced arcs, as shown. Press the seam allowances toward the arc centers.

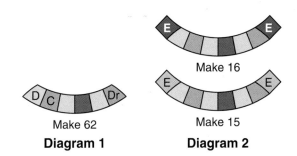

Make 62

Diagram 1

Make 16

Make 15

Diagram 2

3. Before proceeding to assemble the wedding rings, check to make sure that you have a total of 16 long pieced arcs with black/beige plaid E pieces at each end, 15 long pieced arcs with medium plaid E pieces at each end, and 31 remaining short pieced arcs with no E pieces at either end.

4. Referring to **Diagram 3,** sew a short pieced arc to one side of a B piece, placing the striped fabric in the B piece, as shown. Press the seam allowance toward the B piece. Sew a long pieced arc with medium plaid E pieces at the ends to the other side of this B piece, as shown. Repeat to make a total of 15 of these pieced arc units.

Make 15

Diagram 3

5. Referring to **Diagram 4,** make 16 more pieced arc units, placing the medium red striped fabric in the B pieces, as shown, and using the 16 long pieced arcs that have black/beige plaid E pieces at the ends, as shown.

Make 16

Diagram 4

6. Referring to **Diagram 5,** sew four of the pieced arc units from step 5 together with three medium red striped A pieces, forming a row, as shown. Begin and end each of these seams ¼ inch in from the edges of each D and D reverse piece, as indicated by the dots in the diagram. Press the seam allowances toward the A pieces. Make four of these rows.

7. Referring to **Diagram 6,** sew the three pieced arc units that have medium plaid E pieces at the ends at the bottom of one row. Begin and end each of these seams where the E pieces meet the D and D reverse pieces, as indicated by the dots in the diagram. Press the seam allowances toward the A pieces.

8. Referring to **Diagram 7,** sew the seams of the E pieces on adjoining sides of each A piece, as shown. Press these seam allowances in opposite directions. This completes the bottom row of Wedding Rings.

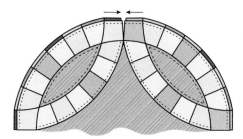

Diagram 7

9. Referring to the **Quilt Diagram,** sew pieced arc units between the remaining rows of Wedding Rings, beginning and ending each of these in the same manner as before. Press the seam allowances toward the A pieces. This allows the E pieces to remain unstitched.

10. Referring to **Diagram 7,** complete the seams at each juncture where two E pieces come together on adjoining sides of an A piece, as shown. Press these seam allowances in opposite directions.

11. Referring to **Diagram 8,** complete the seams at each juncture where four E pieces come together between the Wedding Rings, as shown. Press these seam allowances to one side of the unit.

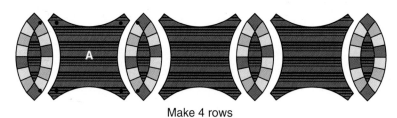

Make 4 rows

Diagram 5

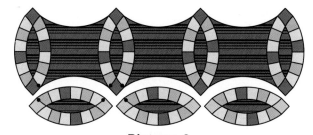

Diagram 6

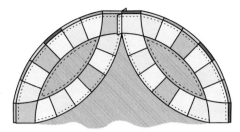

Diagram 8

12. Referring to the **Quilt Diagram,** place the joined Wedding Rings on the dark red print background fabric and appliqué them in place by hand or machine. Use whichever technique you like best. For information on hand and machine appliqué, see pages 157–159.

13. After all of the Wedding Rings have been appliquéd, trim the excess background fabric from behind the Wedding Rings to ¼ inch from the appliquéd stitching. Trimming the excess will allow you to quilt through fewer layers of fabric.

Quilting and Finishing

1. Mark quilting designs as desired. The quilt shown has a spider web quilted in the center of each ring and random leaves quilted between the arcs and around the outer edges of the quilt. It is also quilted in the ditch around the rings, with three added concentric rows of quilting approximately ¼ inch apart around the rings.

2. Layer the quilt top, batting, and back; baste. Trim the back and batting to approximately 3 inches larger than the quilt top on all sides. Quilt all marked quilting designs.

3. From the binding fabric, make approximately 300 inches of double-fold, straight-grain binding. For instructions on making and attaching binding, see page 164.

4. Sew the binding to the quilt top. Trim the excess batting and backing. Using thread to match the binding, hand-sew the folded edge of the binding to the back of the quilt.

Quilt Diagram

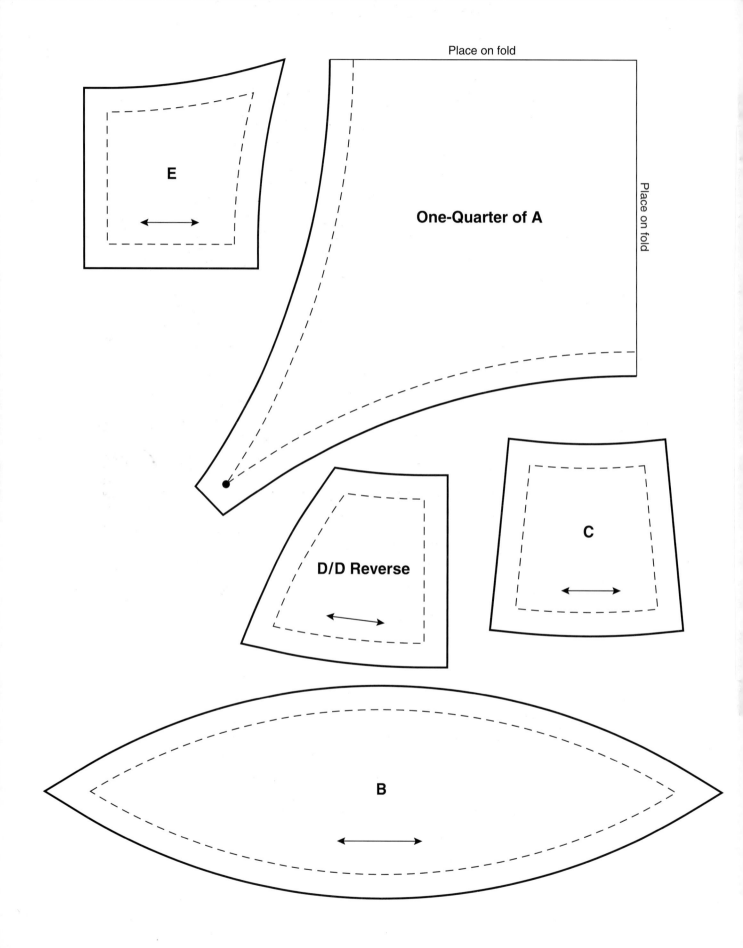

E

Place on fold

One-Quarter of A

Place on fold

D/D Reverse

C

B

Plaid Folk Hearts

Quiltmaker: Roberta Horton

Roberta chose homespun plaid fabrics to make hearts that look as if they were taken from old shirts. The irregular shapes and unfinished edges of her raw-edge appliqué technique create a feeling of exuberance in this delightfully free-spirited folk art quilt. You can give your quilt the same exuberance by cutting freeform hearts from your favorite stripes, plaids, and shirting reproduction fabrics.

Skill Level: Easy

Size: Finished quilt is approximately
　　24 inches × 28½ inches
Finished block is approximately 4½ inches
　　square

Fabrics and Supplies

- ✓ Approximately ½ yard *total* of assorted plaid homespun fabrics for the borders
- ✓ Scraps (*each* approximately 6 inches square) of 40 different homespun fabrics for the blocks and hearts
- ✓ 1 yard of green plaid homespun fabric for the quilt back
- ✓ ¼ yard of red plaid homespun fabric for the binding
- ✓ Crib-size quilt batting (45 × 60 inches)
- ✓ 1 yard of lightweight Tear-Away fabric stabilizer
- ✓ Assorted buttons and ribbons for embellishing the hearts
- ✓ 1 skein of embroidery floss for tying the quilt

Cutting

Except for the appliqués, all measurements include ¼-inch seam allowances. Measurements for the borders are slightly longer than needed; trim them to the exact length when they are added to the quilt top.

From the assorted plaid homespun fabrics, cut:
- Enough 3½-inch-wide strips to piece together four 3½ × 34-inch strips for borders

From the homespun fabric scraps, cut:
- Twenty 5-inch squares for blocks
- 20 heart shapes freehand; see "Hey, I Can Do This!" for information on freehand cutting techniques. **NOTE:** It's a good idea to cut more than 20 hearts, so you can experiment with various color and fabric combinations.
- From the Tear-Away fabric stabilizer, cut twenty 5-inch squares

Appliquéing the Hearts

1. Pin or baste a square of Tear-Away under each 5-inch square of fabric to stabilize it and pin a heart to each block. Refer to the photograph on page 83 for color placement or experiment with your own fabrics on a design surface until you have combinations that please you. Using dark thread or any contrasting color, straight stitch each heart to the block by machine, approximately ¼ inch in from the edge. If the lines of stitching appear uneven, it will only add to the charm of the quilt.

2. Using a combination of straight and zigzag stitches, sew around each heart again. Use a playful approach to these lines, remembering that irregular lines of stitching enhance the free-spirited style of the quilt. You can also use more than one color of thread on each heart; refer to the photograph for more decorative stitching ideas. Carefully remove the Tear-Away from each block after the lines of stitching are complete.

Assembling the Quilt Top

1. Lay out the blocks in five horizontal rows with four blocks in each row. Refer to the photograph on page 83 for color placement or play with different color combinations of your own until you find an arrangement that pleases you.

2. Sew the blocks together in rows, as shown in **Diagram 1.** Press the seams of alternate rows in opposite directions.

Diagram 1

3. Referring to **Diagram 1,** sew the rows together and press the seams in opposite directions.

4. Measure the width of the quilt top and trim the top and bottom border strips to this measurement. Referring to the **Quilt Diagram,** the borders to the top and bottom of the quilt top. Press the seams toward the borders.

5. Measure the length of the quilt top, including borders you just added, and trim the side border strips to this measurement. Referring to the **Quilt Diagram,** sew the borders to the sides of the quilt top. Press the seams toward the borders.

Quilt Diagram

Quilting and Finishing

1. Layer the quilt back, batting, and quilt top; baste. Trim the quilt back so that it is approximately 2 inches larger than the quilt top on all sides.

2. Quilt as desired. The quilt shown is machine quilted in the ditch between blocks. The borders are quilted in a zigzag pattern.

3. From the red homespun fabric, make approximately 130 inches of double-fold binding. See page 164 for instructions on making and attaching binding.

4. Sew the binding to the quilt top. Trim the excess batting and backing, and hand-sew the folded edge of the binding to the back of the quilt.

5. Embellish the hearts with buttons and ribbons, using the photograph on page 83 as a guide. If you choose to do hand quilting, sew the buttons onto the quilt top before layering it. If you do machine quilting, sew the buttons on with embroidery floss after the quilting is finished. Embroidery floss adds to the primitive look of this quilt, and makes it easy to sew the buttons on. Because floss is made up of six individual strands of thread, you may go through each hole of a button just one time. And for a decorative finish, tie the floss into a knot on the back of the quilt.

HEY, I CAN DO THIS!

This quilt offers a chance to loosen up and take a welcome break from the pressure often involved in working with exact seam allowances and precise points. As you cut out the 20 hearts, have fun and don't worry about making them symmetrical. Fold a 4-inch square of fabric in half, cut out a freehand heart, and open it up to inspect your results. Then fold another square of fabric in half and cut the next heart a bit differently. For example, you can make it fatter or more pointed, as shown in the diagram. It's important to make them look different from one another, rather than like they've been cut with a cookie cutter or template. As you become braver, try cutting heart shapes from unfolded squares to create an asymmetrical or lopsided look.

Stargazing with Roberta

Quiltmaker: Karen Hull Sienk

Contemporary plaids from the Roberta Horton collection create a country star quilt made from just two blocks—the Sawtooth Star and Shoo-Fly. Karen's careful attention to placing different color values next to each other have filled this beautiful quilt with sparkle and light. Choose either the bed-size or miniature version to complement your decor.

Skill Level: Easy

Size: Finished quilt is 64½ × 88½ inches
Finished blocks are 8 inches square
(Directions for miniature quilt begin on
page 92.)

Fabrics and Supplies

This quilt contains approximately eight different light background plaids and 18 different medium or dark plaids. The yardages are generous enough to allow for flexibility in cutting and color placement. If you use more or fewer fabrics in your quilt, you may wish to adjust the yardages accordingly. Just for fun, try including some plaids from used men's shirts—or add a few flannel plaids to create intriguing visual texture.

- ✓ 1½ yards of black striped fabric for the outer border
- ✓ 1 yard of assorted white striped and light plaid fabrics for the first and fourth borders
- ✓ ½ yard of blue striped fabric for the second border
- ✓ Assorted dark and medium plaid and striped fabrics *totaling* approximately 3 yards for the blocks and Sawtooth borders
- ✓ Assorted light plaid and striped fabrics *totaling* 2½ yards for the backgrounds in the blocks
- ✓ Full-size batting (81 × 96 inches)
- ✓ 5½ yards of fabric for the quilt back
- ✓ Assorted scraps of dark and medium plaid and striped fabrics for the binding
- ✓ Rotary cutter, ruler, and mat

Cutting

This quilt requires 27 Sawtooth Star blocks and 27 Shoo-Fly blocks, a pieced Sawtooth border, as well as two pieced scrap borders.

Instructions are for quick cutting the pieces with a rotary cutter and ruler. Note that quick cutting may result in leftover pieces. These measurements include ¼-inch seam allowances. Except for the Sawtooth border, the other borders will be longer than needed; trim them to the correct length when adding them to the quilt top.

For the Sawtooth Star Blocks
From the light plaid and striped fabrics, cut:
- Seven 2½ × 45-inch strips. Cut these strips into one hundred eight 2½-inch C squares, in matching sets of 4.
- Four 5¼ × 45-inch strips. Cut these strips into twenty-seven 5¼-inch squares; cut these squares in half diagonally in both directions to make 108 A triangles, in matching sets of 4.

From the medium or dark plaid and striped fabrics, cut:
- Three 4½ × 45-inch strips. Cut these strips into twenty-seven 4½-inch D squares.
- Eight 2⅞ × 45-inch strips. Cut these strips into one hundred eight 2⅞-inch squares. Cut these squares in half diagonally to make 216 B triangles, in matching sets of 8.

For the Shoo-Fly Blocks
From the light plaid and striped fabrics, cut:
- Four 2⅞ × 45-inch strips. Cut these strips into fifty-four 2⅞-inch squares; cut these squares in half diagonally in both directions to make 108 B triangles, in matching sets of 4.

From the medium and dark plaid and striped fabrics, cut:
- Three 4½ × 45-inch strips. Cut these strips into twenty-seven 4½-inch D squares.
- Four 2⅞ × 45-inch strips. Cut these strips into fifty-four 2⅞-inch squares; cut these squares in half diagonally in both directions to make 108 B triangles, in matching sets of 4.
- Thirteen 2½ × 44-inch strips. Cut these strips into 2½ × 4½-inch rectangles. You will need a total of 108 E rectangles in matching sets of 4.

For the Sawtooth Borders
From the light plaid and striped fabrics, cut:
- Two 5¼ × 45-inch strips. Cut these strips into sixteen 5¼-inch squares; cut these squares in half diagonally in both directions to make 64 A triangles.
- Two 2⅞-inch light squares. Cut these squares in half diagonally to make four B triangles.

From the medium and dark plaid and striped fabrics, cut:
- Five 2⅞ × 45-inch strips. Cut these strips into sixty-six 2⅞-inch squares; cut these squares in half diagonally to make 132 B triangles.

From the black striped fabric, cut:
- Two 3½ × 60-inch border strips
- Two 3½ × 90-inch border strips

From the blue striped fabric, cut:
- Two 1½ × 52-inch border strips
- Two 1½ × 78-inch border strips

From the assorted white or light striped and plaid fabrics, cut:
- Thirty 1½ × 9½-inch strips for the first border
- Thirty-four 1½ × 9½-inch strips for the fourth border

From the backing fabric, cut:
- Two 35 × 94-inch pieces

From the assorted scraps of dark and medium plaid and striped fabrics, cut:
- Enough pieces that are 2½ inches wide and various lengths to total approximately 340 inches for the pieced binding.

Piecing the Sawtooth Star Blocks

1. Referring to **Diagram 1,** sew a dark B triangle to each side of an A triangle. Press the seam allowances away from the A triangles. Make a total of 108 of these units, remembering that each Sawtooth Star block requires a set of four of these units that match each other.

Diagram 1

2. Referring to **Diagram 2,** sew a C square to each end of one unit, as shown. Each Sawtooth Star block requires four matching C squares. Make a total of 54 of these rows. Reserve the remaining 54 units for the sides of the Sawtooth Star block.

Diagram 2

3. Referring to the **Sawtooth Star Block Diagram,** sew two of the units from Step 1 to each

side of a D center square, as shown. Sew two of the rows with C corner squares to the top and bottom edges, completing the Sawtooth Star block, as shown.

4. Make 27 Sawtooth Star blocks.

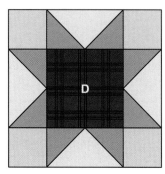

Sawtooth Star Block Diagram

Piecing the Shoo-Fly Blocks

1. Referring to **Diagram 3,** sew a light B triangle to a dark B triangle, as shown. Press the seam allowances toward the darker fabric. Each Shoo-Fly block requires four sets of these light/dark triangle-pieced squares in matching fabrics.

2. Referring to **Diagram 4,** sew two matching triangle-pieced B squares to an E rectangle, as shown. Press the seam allowances toward the E rectangle. Each Shoo-Fly block requires two of these rows in matching fabrics.

Diagram 3   **Diagram 4**

3. Referring to **Diagram 5,** sew an E rectangle that matches the rectangle used in Step 2 to each side of a D center square, as shown. Press the seam allowances toward the E rectangles.

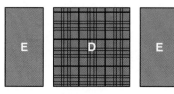

Diagram 5

4. Referring to the **Shoo-Fly Block Diagram,** sew the three rows together, completing the Shoo-Fly block. Make 27 Shoo-Fly blocks.

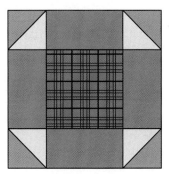

Shoo-Fly Block Diagram

Assembling the Quilt Top

1. Referring to the **Quilt Diagram** on page 90 for block placement, sew the Sawtooth Star and Shoo-Fly blocks together into nine horizontal rows of six blocks each. Press the seam allowances in opposite directions between blocks.

2. Referring to the **Quilt Diagram,** sew the nine horizontal rows of blocks together. Press the seam allowances in alternate directions between rows.

Making and Attaching the Borders

Piecing the First Border

1. Sew together six light 1½ × 9½-inch rectangles to form the top and bottom inner scrap borders. Press the seam allowances to one side.

2. Sew together nine 1½ × 9½-inch rectangles to form the side inner scrap borders. Press the seam allowances to one side.

3. Referring to the **Quilt Diagram** on page 90, sew the top and bottom inner scrap borders to the quilt top, trimming the ends of the borders even with the edge of the quilt top. Press the seam allowances toward the borders.

4. In the same manner, sew the side inner scrap borders to the quilt top and trim them even with the edges of the quilt top. Press the seam allowances toward the borders.

Attaching the Second Border

1. Sew the two 1½ × 52-inch blue striped border strips to the top and bottom edges of the quilt top, trimming them even with the edges of the quilt top. Press the seam allowances toward these borders.

2. Sew the two 1½ × 78-inch blue striped border strips to the sides of the quilt top, trimming them in the same manner. Press the seam allowances toward these borders.

Piecing the Sawtooth Borders

1. Referring to **Diagram 1,** sew a dark or medium B triangle to each side of an A triangle, as shown. The Sawtooth border requires a total of 64 of these light/dark triangle-pieced units.

2. Referring to the **Sawtooth Border Diagram,** sew together a row of 13 triangle-pieced units for each of the top and bottom Sawtooth borders. Press the seam allowances to one side.

3. Sew these top and bottom Sawtooth borders to the top and bottom edges of the quilt top. Press the seam allowances toward the blue striped borders.

4. Referring to the **Sawtooth Border Diagram,** sew together a row of 19 triangle-pieced units for each side Sawtooth border. Press the seam allowances to one side.

Top and Bottom Borders

Side Borders

Sawtooth Border Diagram

Quilt Diagram

5. Referring to **Diagram 3** on page 88, sew a light B triangle to a dark B triangle, as shown. Repeat to make three more of these triangle-pieced B squares. Sew a light/dark B triangle-pieced square to each end of the side Sawtooth borders. Press the seam allowances to one side.

6. Sew these side Sawtooth borders to the sides of the quilt top. Press the seam allowances toward the second borders.

Piecing the Fourth Border

1. Referring to the **Quilt Diagram,** sew seven light plaid or striped 1½ × 9½-inch rectangles to-gether for the pieced scrap outer borders that will be sewn to the top and bottom edges of the quilt top. Press the seam allowances to one side.

2. Referring to the **Quilt Diagram,** sew to-gether ten light plaid or striped 1½ × 9½-inch rectangles for the pieced scrap outer borders that will be sewn to the sides of the quilt top. Press the seam allowances to one side.

3. Sew the top and bottom pieced scrap outer borders to the quilt top, trimming the ends of the borders even with the edge of the quilt top. Press the seam allowances toward these borders.

4. Sew the side pieced scrap outer borders to the quilt top, trimming the ends of the borders in the same manner. Press the seam allowances toward these borders.

Attaching the Outer Borders

1. Sew the two 3½ × 60-inch black striped border strips to the top and bottom edges of the quilt top and trim them even with the edge of the quilt top. Press the seam allowances toward the black striped borders.

2. Sew the two 3½ × 90-inch black striped border strips to the side edges of the quilt top, trimming them in the same manner. Press the seam allowances toward the black striped borders.

Quilting and Finishing

1. Mark quilting designs as desired. The Sawtooth and Shoo-Fly blocks in the quilt shown are quilted as indicated in the **Quilting Diagram.** The first and second borders are quilted ¼ inch away from the outer edges. The Sawtooth border is quilted ¼ inch away from the pieced triangle units. The fourth and outer borders are quilted in straight lines at 2-inch intervals and have diagonal lines of quilting at the corners that give these borders the visual illusion of mitered seams.

2. Trim the selvages from the two pieces of backing fabric and sew them together along the long edge. Press this seam open.

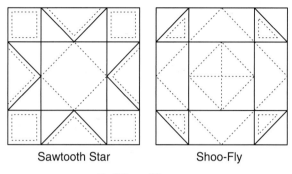

Sawtooth Star   Shoo-Fly

Quilting Diagram

3. Layer the quilt back, batting, and quilt top; baste. Trim the quilt back and batting 3 inches larger than the quilt top on all sides.

4. Quilt all marked quilting designs and add any additional quilting designs desired.

5. Place the binding strips together, end to end, alternating shorter strips with longer strips. Sew the strips together with diagonal seams to create approximately 320 inches of decorative binding. Press the seams open and trim them to ¼ inch, if necessary, to reduce bulk in the binding.

6. Sew the binding to the quilt top. Hand-sew the folded edge of the binding to the back of the quilt. For more information on making and attaching binding, see page 164.

Stargazing with Roberta Miniature

Size: Finished quilt is 32 × 40 inches
Finished blocks are 4 inches square
(shown in the photograph on page 83)

Fabrics and Supplies

This quilt requires approximately eight different light or medium plaid or striped fabrics and 18 different medium or dark plaid or striped fabrics. Instructions are for quick cutting the pieces with a rotary cutter and ruler. These measurements include ¼-inch seam allowances. The yardages are generous enough to allow for flexibility in cutting and color placement. If you decide to use more or fewer fabrics in your quilt, you may wish to adjust the yardages accordingly.

- ✓ ¾ yard of black striped fabric for the outer borders
- ✓ ⅓ yard of white striped fabric for the first and third borders
- ✓ ¼ yard of red striped fabric for the second border
- ✓ Assorted dark and medium plaid and striped fabrics *totaling* approximately 1½ yards for the blocks and Sawtooth borders
- ✓ Assorted light plaid and striped fabrics *totaling* approximately 1 yard for the backgrounds in the blocks
- ✓ 1¼ yards of fabric for the quilt back
- ✓ Crib-size batting (45 × 60 inches)
- ✓ Rotary cutter, ruler, and mat

Cutting

This quilt requires 18 Sawtooth Star blocks, 17 Shoo-Fly blocks, and one Sawtooth border, in addition to the four other borders. Instructions are for quick cutting the pieces with a rotary cutter and ruler. Note that quick cutting may result in leftover pieces. These measurements include ¼-inch seam allowances. Except for the Sawtooth border, the borders will be longer than needed; trim them to the correct length when adding them to the quilt top.

For the Sawtooth Star Blocks
From the light plaid and striped fabrics, cut:
- Three 1½ × 45-inch strips. Cut these strips into seventy-two 1½-inch C squares, in matching sets of 4.
- Two 3¼ × 45-inch strips. Cut these strips into eighteen 3¼-inch squares; cut these squares in half diagonally in both directions to make 72 A triangles, in matching sets of 4.

From the dark plaid and striped fabrics, cut:
- Two 2½ × 45-inch strips. Cut these strips into eighteen 2½-inch D squares.
- Two 1⅞ × 45-inch strips. Cut theses strips into thirty-six 1⅞-inch squares; cut these squares in half diagonally in both directions to make 144 B triangles, in matching sets of 8.

For the Shoo-Fly Blocks
From the light or medium plaid and striped fabrics, cut:
- Seventeen 1⅞-inch squares. Cut these squares in half diagonally in both directions to make 68 B triangles, in matching sets of 4.

From the medium or dark plaid or striped fabrics, cut:
- One 1⅞ × 45-inch strip. Cut this strip into seventeen 1⅞-inch squares; cut these squares in half diagonally in both directions to make 68 B triangles, in matching sets of 4.
- Five 1½ × 45-inch strips. Cut these strips into sixty-eight 1½ × 2½-inch E rectangles, in matching sets of 4.
- Two 2½ × 45-inch strips. Cut these strips into seventeen 2½-inch D squares.

For the Sawtooth Borders

From the light or medium plaid or striped fabrics, cut:

- Two 3¼ × 45-inch strips. Cut these strips into thirteen 3¼-inch squares; cut these squares in half diagonally in both directions to make 52 A triangles.
- Two 1⅞-inch squares. Cut these squares in half diagonally for to make 4 B triangles.

From the medium or dark plaid or striped fabrics, cut:

- One 1⅞ × 45-inch strip. Cut this strip into fourteen 1⅞-inch squares; cut these squares in half diagonally to make 56 B triangles.

From the black striped fabric, cut:

- Two 3½ × 26½-inch top and bottom border strips
- Two 3½ × 40½-inch side border strips

From the white striped fabric, cut:

- Two 1½ × 24½-inch top and bottom border strips
- Two 1½ × 35½-inch side border strips
- Two 1 × 20½-inch top and bottom border strips
- Two 1 × 29½-inch side border strips

From the red striped fabric, cut:

- Two 1½ × 31½-inch top and bottom border strips
- Two 1¼ × 22½-inch side border strips

From the assorted scraps of dark and medium plaid and striped fabrics, cut:

- Enough pieces 2½ inches wide and of varying lengths to total approximately 180 inches for the binding.

Piecing the Sawtooth Star Blocks

1. Follow the same piecing sequence for the larger Sawtooth Star blocks. This is described on page 88.

2. Make a total of eighteen 4-inch Sawtooth Star blocks for this miniature version of Stargazing with Roberta.

Piecing the Shoo-Fly Blocks

1. Follow the same piecing sequence for the larger Shoo-Fly blocks. This is described on pages 88 and 89.

2. Make a total of seventeen 4-inch Sawtooth Star blocks for this miniature quilt.

Assembling the Quilt Top

Referring to the **Quilt Diagram** for block placement, sew the Sawtooth Star and Shoo-Fly blocks together into seven horizontal rows of five blocks each, as shown.

Quilt Diagram

Piecing the Sawtooth Borders

1. Follow the same piecing sequence for the larger basic border triangle unit, as shown on pages 88 and 89.

2. Referring to the **Quilt Diagram,** sew together 15 of these triangle units for each of the two side Sawtooth borders, as shown. Press the seam allowances to one side.

3. Sew together 11 of these triangle-pieced units for each of the top and bottom Sawtooth borders.

4. Referring to **Diagram 3** on page 88, sew a light B triangle to a dark B triangle, as shown. Repeat to make three more of these triangle-pieced B squares. Sew a light/dark B triangle-pieced square to each end of the side Sawtooth borders. Press the seam allowances to one side.

Attaching the Borders to the Quilt Top

The borders on this quilt are slightly different from those for the larger version. Refer to the **Quilt Diagram** on page 93 as you attach each of the borders to the quilt top and press all seam allowances toward the border strips, unless otherwise specified.

1. Sew the white striped 1 × 20½-inch top and bottom border strips to the top and bottom edges of the quilt top.

2. Sew the white striped 1 × 29½-inch side border strips to the side edges of the quilt top.

3. Sew the red striped 1½ × 31½-inch top and bottom border strips to the top and bottom edges of the quilt top.

4. Sew the red striped 1¼ × 22½-inch side border strips to the side edges of the quilt top.

5. Sew the top and bottom Sawtooth borders to the top and bottom edges of the quilt top. Press the seams toward the red borders.

6. Sew the side Sawtooth borders to the side edges of the quilt top. Press these seam allowances toward the red borders.

7. Sew the white striped 1½ × 24½-inch top and bottom border strips to the top and bottom edges of the quilt top. Press these seam allowances toward the red borders.

8. Sew the white striped 1½ × 35½-inch side border strips to the side edges of the quilt top. Press the seams toward the red borders.

9. Sew the top and bottom black striped border strips to the top and bottom edges of the quilt top.

10. Sew the side black striped border strips to the sides of the quilt top.

Quilting and Finishing

1. Mark quilting designs as desired. The Sawtooth and Shoo-Fly blocks in the quilt shown are quilted as indicated in the **Quilting Diagram.** The first white striped borders are quilted in a straight line through the center. The red striped borders are quilted ¼ inch from the inner edges. The Sawtooth borders are quilted in the ditch along each A triangle. The fourth and outer borders are quilted ¼ inch from the inner edges, and there are straight lines of quilting that extend from the seams between each of the B triangles in the Sawtooth borders to the outer edges of the quilt.

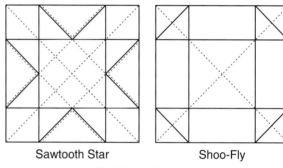

Sawtooth Star   Shoo-Fly

Quilting Diagram

2. Layer the quilt top, batting and back; baste. Trim the excess back and batting to approximately 3 inches larger than the quilt top.

3. Quilt all marked quilting designs and add any additional quilting desired.

4. Place the binding strips together, end to end, shorter strips alternating with longer strips. Sew the strips together with diagonal seams to create approximately 160 inches of decorative binding. Press these seams open and trim them to ¼ inch to reduce bulk in the binding.

5. Attach the binding to the quilt top. Hand-sew the folded edge of the binding to the back of the quilt. For more information on making and attaching binding, see page 164.

Escargot in Plaid

Quiltmaker: Shelby Morris

Shelby's sense of humor—and adventure—bubbles to the surface in this lively interpretation of the traditional Snail's Trail pattern. A wealth of plaid fabrics lends a country flavor to this easy-to-piece quilt. Use your rotary cutter and sewing machine to make one for your favorite teenager.

Skill Level: Easy

Size: Finished quilt is 85½ × 97½ inches
Finished block is 12 inches square

Fabrics and Supplies

- ✓ 2¾ yards of subtle beige check for the blocks, inner border, and binding
- ✓ 1¼ yards of a single dark brown plaid for the blocks and pieced border
- ✓ ¼ yard *each* of 28 different light plaid fabrics for the blocks and pieced border. These may be either regular (9 × 44-inch) or fat (18 × 22-inch) quarters
- ✓ Scraps (approximately 10 × 18 inches *each*) of 29 different dark plaid fabrics for the blocks and pieced border
- ✓ 3 yards of 90-inch-wide muslin or 6 yards of 45-inch-wide muslin for the quilt back
- ✓ Queen-size quilt batting (90 × 108 inches)
- ✓ Rotary cutter, ruler, and mat

Cutting

The instructions for this quilt are written for quick-cutting the blocks and borders using a rotary cutter and ruler. Quick-piecing methods are included where applicable. Note that for some of the pieces, the quick-cutting method may result in leftovers. All measurements include ¼-inch seam allowances. Measurements for the borders are longer than needed. Trim them to the exact length when they are added to the quilt top. Cut pieces in the following sequence.

From the beige check, cut:
- Nine 2 × 44-inch strips for binding
- Two 9 × 74-inch inner border strips
- Two 9 × 80-inch inner border strips
- Two 6⅞-inch squares. Cut these squares in half diagonally to make 4 D triangles.
- Two 5⅛-inch squares. Cut these squares in half diagonally to make 4 C triangles.
- Two 3⅞-inch squares. Cut these squares in half diagonally to make 4 B triangles
- One 2⅝ × 11-inch strip. Cut this strip into 2⅝-inch squares to make a total of 4 A squares.

From the dark brown plaid, cut:
- One 4¾-inch strip on the lengthwise grain. Cut this strip into 4¾-inch E squares. You will need a total of 4 E squares.
- Fourteen 2⅝-inch strips on the cross grain of the fabric. Cut these strips into 2⅝ × 17-inch strips. You will need a total of 28 of these strips.
- One 6⅞-inch square. Cut this square in half diagonally to make 2 D triangles.
- One 5⅛-inch square. Cut this square in half diagonally to make 2 C triangles.
- One 3⅞-inch square. Cut this square in half diagonally to make 2 B triangles.
- One 2⅝ × 6-inch strip

From each of the light plaid fabrics, cut:
NOTE: If you are cutting from a regular quarter yard of fabric, cut in the order shown. If you are cutting from a fat quarter, cut the longest strip first.

- One 6⅞-inch square. Cut this square in half diagonally to make 2 D triangles.
- One 5⅛-inch square. Cut this square in half diagonally to make 2 C triangles.
- One 3⅞-inch square. Cut this square in half diagonally to make 2 B triangles.
- One 2⅝ × 17-inch strip
- One 2⅝ × 6-inch strip

From each of the 29 dark plaid scraps, cut:
- One 6⅞-inch square. Cut this square in half diagonally to make 2 D triangles.
- One 5⅛-inch square. Cut this square in half diagonally to make 2 C triangles.
- One 3⅞-inch square. Cut this square in half diagonally to make 2 B triangles.
- One 2⅝ × 6-inch strip

Piecing the Blocks

This quilt requires a total of 30 pieced blocks as shown in the **Block Diagram.** Each block includes one light plaid and one dark plaid fabric. Referring to the photograph on page 95, note that two of the blocks use the beige check as the light fabric for pieces A, B, C, and D.

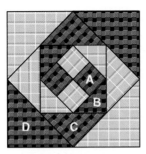

Block Diagram

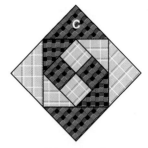

Diagram 2   **Diagram 3**

1. Referring to **Diagram 1,** sew two contrasting (light/dark) $2\frac{5}{8} \times 6$-inch strips along the long edge. Press the seam allowance toward the darker fabric.

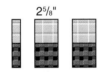

2⅝"

Diagram 1

2. Cut the newly created light/dark strip into two $2\frac{5}{8}$-inch "slices," as shown in **Diagram 1.**

3. Pair the "slices" as shown in the **Four Patch Diagram,** taking care to pin carefully. Because the seam allowances are pressed in opposite directions, the seams will "nest" nicely for a clean match. After stitching, press the seam allowance to one side.

Four Patch Diagram

4. Using the same light and dark plaids, sew a light B triangle to opposite sides of the four patch, as shown in **Diagram 2.** Then sew a dark B triangle to each of the remaining sides, as shown. Press the seam allowances away from the center of the block.

5. Again using the same light and dark plaids, sew a light C triangle to opposite sides of the block, as shown in **Diagram 3.** Sew a dark C triangle to each of the remaining sides, as shown. Press the seam allowances away from the center of the block.

6. Continuing with the same lights and darks, sew a light D triangle to opposite sides of the block, as shown in **Diagram 4.** Sew a dark D triangle to each of the remaining sides, as shown, to complete the block. Press the seam allowances away from the center of the block.

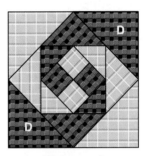

Diagram 4

Assembling the Quilt Top

1. Lay out the blocks in six horizontal rows of five blocks each, referring to the **Quilt Diagram** on page 98 for proper positioning. Note that the lights and darks in each block are rotated in groups of four, as shown in **Diagram 5.** Also note that the blocks containing the beige border fabric are positioned in the upper and lower left corners. They will appear to "float" when the inner borders are attached.

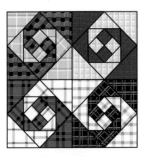

Diagram 5

Quilt Diagram

2. Sew the five blocks in each horizontal row together, pressing the seam allowances between blocks in opposite directions from row to row.

3. Sew the six rows of blocks together, carefully aligning the seams. Press the seam allowances toward the top edge of the quilt top.

Assembling and Attaching the Inner Border

1. Sew the remaining dark D triangles in "non-matching" pairs along a short side, as shown in

Diagram 6. Make a total of five D triangle-pieced units. Press the seam allowances under on the two short sides and prepare them for appliqué by basting them in place if you wish.

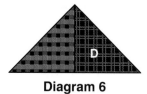

Diagram 6

2. Take the lengthwise measurement of the quilt top. Trim the 9 × 74-inch beige check inner border strips to this measurement and crease them at the midpoints. Match the midpoint of one trimmed border strip with the midpoint of the left side of the quilt top. Pin or baste one of the five D triangle-pieced units in place on the border strip as indicated in the **Quilt Diagram,** aligning the raw edges. With right sides together, pin the border to the quilt, taking care to match the midpoints and appropriate seams. Stitch the border to the quilt top. The raw edge of the D triangle-pieced unit will be caught and hidden in the seam.

3. Repeat the process, using the remaining 9 × 74-inch beige border and two D triangle-pieced units on the right side of the quilt top. Refer to the **Quilt Diagram** for placement.

4. Take the crosswise measurement of the quilt top and trim the 9 × 80-inch borders to this measurement. Position one of the remaining D triangle-pieced units on each border, referring to the **Quilt Diagram** for placement. Sew these borders to the top and bottom of the quilt, following the procedure in Step 2.

5. Appliqué the short sides of the D triangle units to each border, using a blind hem stitch and thread to match the triangles. For more information about hand appliqué, see page 157.

Assembling and Attaching the Outer Border

The outer border requires a total of 78 four-patch units. The consistent fabric in each is the dark brown plaid.

1. Pair a 2⅝ × 17-inch dark brown plaid strip with a light plaid strip of matching size. Sew them together lengthwise, taking care to maintain a consistent ¼-inch seam. Press the seam allowance toward the dark fabric. Make a total of 28 light/dark brown strips.

2. Cut each light/dark strip into six 2⅝-inch "slices" and sew together three four patch units from each set of slices. There will be a total of 84 four patch units, giving you a few extra units to play with!

> ## SEW IN BATCHES
>
> The pieced borders will be more accurate if you stitch the four patch units together in groups of three, then six, rather than building one long, continuous chain of units.

3. Join the four patch units into two border strips of 18 units each. Mix the units randomly, so that like four patches do not lie side by side. Make two additional border strips of 21 units each.

4. Mark the midpoint of each pieced border strip with a pin. Matching edges and midpoints with the beige inner border, sew an 18-unit border strip to the top and bottom of the quilt top. You may stretch or ease the pieced border slightly, or if the adjustment is too great, take deeper (or narrower) seams in a few of the four patch units to make up the difference.

5. Sew an E square to each end of the remaining (21-unit) border strips and sew these borders to the left and right sides of the quilt top.

Quilting and Finishing

1. Mark quilting designs as desired. The quilt shown is quilted in a diagonal grid that extends into the beige inner border. To mark the lines of this grid, draw lines outward from the center of a block and simply extend them into the adjacent blocks. The four patch border is quilted in the ditch.

2. Layer the quilt backing, batting and quilt top; baste. Trim the backing and batting to approximately 3 inches beyond all sides of the quilt top. Quilt all marked designs.

3. Sew the 2 × 44-inch beige strips together to make approximately 375 inches of double-fold binding.

4. Sew the binding to the quilt top. Trim the excess batting and backing, and hand-sew the folded edge of the binding to the back of the quilt. For more instructions on making and attaching binding, see page 164.

Plaid Spools

Quiltmaker: Kim Baird

A delightful mixture of plaid, print, and solid fabrics works with great success in this bright quilt, perfect for the wall of any dedicated quilter's sewing room. If you've never tried your hand at set-in pieces, you'll find the technique given for marking fabric a surefire way to achieve crisp corners for these set-in pieces.

Skill Level: Intermediate

Size: Finished quilt is 40 × 44 inches. Finished block is 4½ inches square

Fabrics and Supplies

A different plaid fabric was used for each of the 56 blocks in the quilt shown. In approximately half of the blocks, the center A square matches the plaid used for the spool; in the remaining blocks, a solid or print was used for the center square. Many of the solid fabrics used for the background, such as the dark gold, bright yellow gold, bright yellow, and light yellow, were used more than once. When selecting fabrics for each block, choose a plaid and a solid that contrast well with each other. The yardage amounts listed below are generous estimates and represent the total amount needed.

- ✓ ½ yard of plaid fabric for outer border
- ✓ ¼ yard of dark green solid fabric for inner border
- ✓ 1½ yards *total* of assorted solid-color fabrics (dark gold, bright yellow gold, bright yellow, and light yellow) for block background and center A squares
- ✓ 1½ yards *total* of assorted plaid fabrics for B and C pieces in blocks
- ✓ An assortment of 2-inch-wide strips that total at least 56 inches in length in several medium-to-dark solids (olive, brown, navy, rust, teal, royal blue, black, and green) for center A squares on some blocks (optional)
- ✓ 1½ yards of fabric for quilt back
- ✓ ½ yard of solid tan fabric for binding
- ✓ Crib-size quilt batting (45 × 60 inches)
- ✓ Rotary cutter, ruler, and mat

Cutting

Instructions given are for rotary-cutting all pieces. **Note:** If you prefer to cut A and B pieces with scissors, use templates A and B on page 103 to mark fabric for cutting. Border strips will be slightly longer than needed; trim them to the exact length when they are added to the quilt top.

From the plaid border fabric, cut:
- Four 3½ × 44-inch strips for outer borders

From the dark green solid fabric, cut:
- Four 1¾ × 44-inch strips for inner borders

From the various yellow and gold fabrics, cut:
- Seventeen 2 × 42-inch strips for solid B trapezoid pieces. For a scrappier mix, cut an equivalent length of shorter strips. Referring to the **Trapezoid Cutting Diagram** on the next page, use a rotary ruler to cut a 45-degree edge on the left end of a strip. Beginning at the tip of the angled edge, measure and mark a 5¾-inch segment. Align your ruler with the mark to cut a second 45-degree angle that's a mirror image of the first. Repeat to cut a total of 112 B pieces.

From the various plaid fabrics, cut:
- An assortment of 2-inch-wide strips totaling at least 56 inches in length. Cut the strips into twenty-eight 2-inch A squares.
- Seventeen 2 × 42-inch strips for plaid B pieces. Cut 112 B pieces from plaids using the same technique shown on page 102 as for yellow and gold fabrics. Cut even numbers of each plaid if you want fabrics within individual blocks to match.

From the medium and dark solid fabrics, cut:
- An assortment of 2-inch-wide strips totaling at least 56 inches in length. Cut the strips into twenty-eight 2-inch A squares.

Piecing Helpers

Make piecing-helper templates for A and B using the patterns on page 103. Use a sewing machine needle to make holes in the templates at the corner dots shown in the patterns. Align the templates on the wrong side of each A and B piece. Mark the dots on the fabric through the corner holes. The dots will make setting-in the pieces easier.

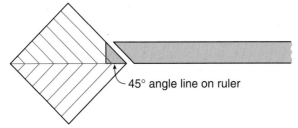

Make a 45° cut at the left end of the strip

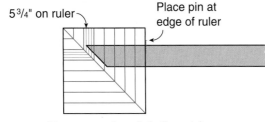

5 3/4" on ruler

Place pin at
edge of ruler

Measure and mark (with a pin)
5 3/4" from top tip of strip.

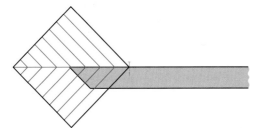

Align tip of ruler with the pin
and cut a second 45° angle.

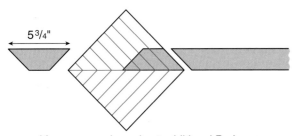

5 3/4"

Measure, mark, and cut additional B pieces

Trapezoid Cutting Diagram

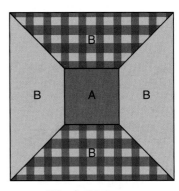

Block Diagram

matching solid color B pieces, as shown in the **Block Diagram**.

2. Pin a plaid B piece to one side of the A square, pin-matching at the marked dots. Start stitching at one dot and continue to the end dot, backstitching at the beginning and end of the seam. Do not sew into the seam allowance at either end. In the same manner, pin and join the other plaid B piece to the opposite side of the square.

3. Set in each of the two solid B pieces by sewing three separate seams, as indicated in **Diagram 1**. Begin by pin-matching one side of a solid B piece to the adjacent side of the plaid B piece. Stitch from the outside raw edge to the inner dot, backstitching at the beginning and end of the seam; do not stitch into the seam allowance. Pin-match the middle side of the solid B piece to the A square, and stitch from dot to dot. Pin and sew the third seam, stitching from the inner dot to the outside raw edge. Repeat for the other solid B piece. Press the seams away from the center square.

4. Repeat in the same manner to make a total of 56 blocks.

Piecing the Blocks

1. For each block, lay out two matching plaid B pieces, a center A square that either matches or contrasts with the plaid B pieces, and two

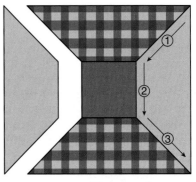

Sew seams
in the order
shown

Diagram 1

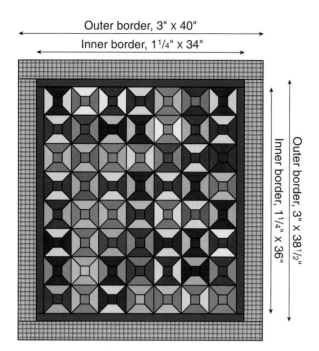

Outer border, 3" x 40"
Inner border, 1¼" x 34"

Outer border, 3" x 38½"
Inner border, 1¼" x 36"

Quilt Diagram

Assembling the Quilt Top

1. Referring to the **Quilt Diagram**, lay out the 56 completed blocks in eight horizontal rows of seven blocks per row as shown.

2. Join the blocks into rows. Press the seams in alternate directions from row to row. Join the rows.

3. Measure the length of the quilt top (approximately 36½ inches). Trim two of the dark green solid border strips to this length, and sew them to the sides of the quilt top. Measure the width of the quilt top (approximately 34½ inches). Trim and add the two remaining green border strips.

4. Measure the length of the quilt top (approximately 39 inches); trim two plaid border strips to length and add them to the sides of the quilt. Measure the width of the quilt top (approximately 40½ inches); trim the remaining plaid border strips, and add them to the top and bottom.

Quilting and Finishing

1. Mark quilting designs as desired. The blocks in the quilt shown were quilted as illustrated in **Diagram 2**. In addition, a diagonal grid of 1¼-inch squares was quilted in the borders.

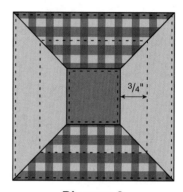

¾"

Diagram 2

2. Layer the quilt back, batting, and quilt top; baste. Trim the quilt back so it is approximately 2 to 3 inches larger than the quilt top on all sides.

3. Quilt as desired.

4. From the tan binding fabric, make approximately 175 inches of double-fold binding. See page 164 for suggested binding widths and instructions on making and attaching binding.

5. Sew the binding to the quilt top. Trim the excess batting and backing, and hand-sew the folded edge of the binding to the back of the quilt.

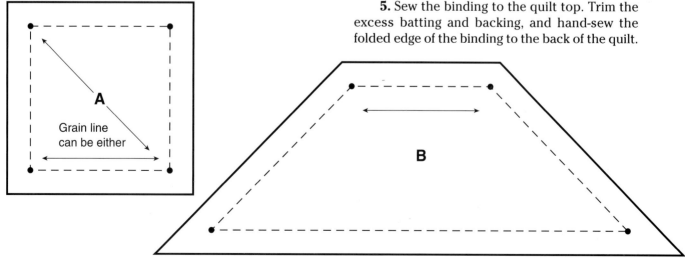

A

Grain line
can be either

B

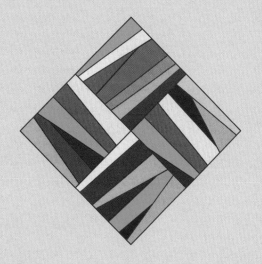

Lights, Brights, & Darks

∎

Baskets of Love

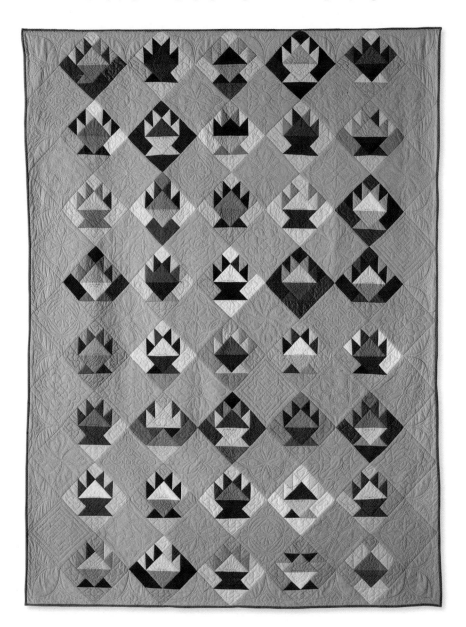

Quiltmaker: Connie Rodman

This quilt began as a wedding gift of 38 hand-pieced Cactus Basket blocks presented to Connie by her quilt club. She pieced two more blocks, then set them together using solid fabrics in desert colors that she felt fit the color theme of the quilt. Over 20 different hand-quilted designs add to the simple beauty of this quilt.

Skill Level: Easy

Size: Finished quilt is 84¾ × 113 inches
Finished block is 10 inches square (approximately 14⅛ inches on the diagonal)

Fabrics and Supplies

- ✓ 3½ yards of medium peach solid fabric for setting squares
- ✓ 2 yards of medium green solid fabric for setting triangles
- ✓ Fat quarters (18 × 22-inch rectangles), or the equivalent in scraps, of 20 to 25 different solid color fabrics for patchwork (Light, medium, and dark shades of colors such as blue, green, gold, pink, purple, rust, burgundy, and brown were used in the quilt shown.)
- ✓ ¾ yard of mauve solid fabric for binding
- ✓ 7⅞ yards of fabric for quilt back
- ✓ King-size quilt batting (120 inches square)
- ✓ Rotary cutter, ruler, and mat
- ✓ Template plastic (optional)

Cutting

All measurements include a ¼-inch seam allowance. The cutting instructions that follow give directions for quick-cutting the pieces with a rotary cutter and ruler. Cut all strips across the fabric width.

You may want to cut just enough pieces to make one block to test your cutting and seam allowances for accuracy. If your finished block does not measure the size stated above, you can make adjustments in your seam allowances before cutting all your fabric.

From the medium peach solid fabric, cut:
- Forty-two 10½-inch setting squares: Cut eleven 10½-inch strips. Cut the strips into 10½-inch squares.

From the medium green solid fabric, cut:
- 28 side setting triangles: Cut four 15⅜-inch strips. Cut the strips into seven 15⅜-inch

squares. Cut each square in half diagonally in both directions to make four triangles.

From the assorted solid color fabrics, cut a total of:
- 400 A triangles: Cut thirty-four 3⅜-inch strips. From the strips, cut 200 squares, each 3⅜ inches square. Cut each square in half diagonally to make two triangles.
- 40 B squares: Cut six 3-inch strips. Cut the strips into 3-inch squares.
- 120 C triangles: Cut twenty 5⅞-inch strips. Cut the strips into 60 squares, each 5⅞ inches square. Cut each square in half diagonally to make two triangles.
- 80 D rectangles: Cut twenty 3-inch strips. Cut the strips into 3 × 5½-inch rectangles.

Piecing the Blocks

For each block you will need ten A triangles, one B square, three C triangles, and two D rectangles. Choose the pieces randomly for each block so that no two blocks are the same; however, it's a good idea to make sure you have good contrast between parts of the block, such as the pairs of A triangles and the two C triangles that make up the center of the block.

1. Stitch four pairs of A triangles together along the long edges to make four triangle-square units as shown in **Diagram 1.**

Diagram 1

2. Sew the triangle-squares together in pairs referring to **Diagram 2** for diagonal line placement. As shown, add a B square to the end of one of the triangle-square pairs, being sure to note the position of the diagonal lines. Press the seam toward the square.

Diagram 2

3. Join two C triangles along their long edges to make a large triangle-square. Sew the pair of A triangle-squares to the C unit as shown in **Diagram 3.** Press the seam toward the C unit.

Diagram 3

4. Sew the triangle-squares with the attached B square to the side of the C unit as shown in **Diagram 4.**

Diagram 4

5. Sew the remaining two A triangles to the D rectangles as shown in **Diagram 5.** Sew these pieces to adjacent sides of the block as shown. Press the seams toward the side pieces.

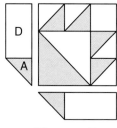

Diagram 5

6. Add a C triangle to complete the block as shown in **Diagram 6.** Press the seam toward the triangle. Repeat to make 40 basket blocks.

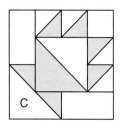

Diagram 6

Assembling the Quilt Top

1. Referring to the **Quilt Diagram,** lay out the blocks, setting squares, and side setting triangles in a pleasing color arrangement.

2. Join the blocks and setting pieces into diagonal rows. The heavy lines on the diagram indicate the rows. Press the seams toward the setting pieces.

3. Stitch the rows together, aligning the seam intersections.

Quilting and Finishing

1. Mark quilting designs. Among the quilting designs used on the quilt shown are a feathered heart motif in the center of the basket blocks and a triple heart design in the setting triangles. A variety of quilting designs were used in the plain setting squares. The two heart motifs and one of the quilting designs used in the setting squares are provided on pages 110–111. All seams are outline quilted.

2. Cut the backing fabric into three equal lengths and trim away selvages. Sew the three pieces together along the long edges. Press the seams away from the center panel. The seams will run parallel to the width of the quilt top.

3. Layer the quilt back, batting, and quilt top; baste. Trim the quilt back and batting so they are approximately 3 inches larger than the quilt top on all sides.

4. Quilt all marked designs.

5. From the binding fabric, make approximately 420 inches of double-fold binding. See page 164 for suggested binding widths and instructions on making and attaching binding.

6. Sew the binding to the quilt top. Trim the excess batting and backing, and hand-sew the folded edge of the binding to the wrong side of the quilt.

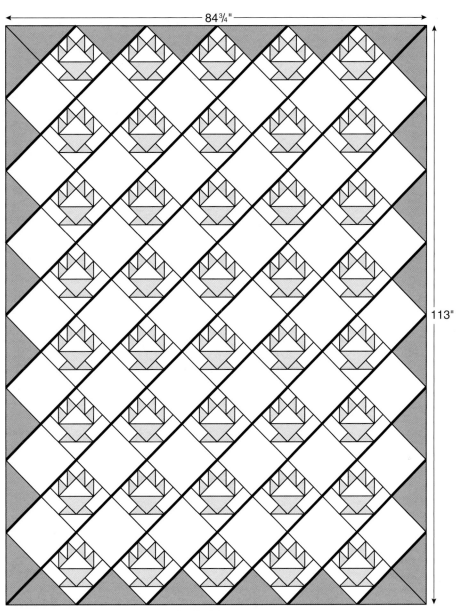

84¾"

113"

Quilt Diagram

**Feathered Heart Quilting Design
for Center of Basket Blocks**

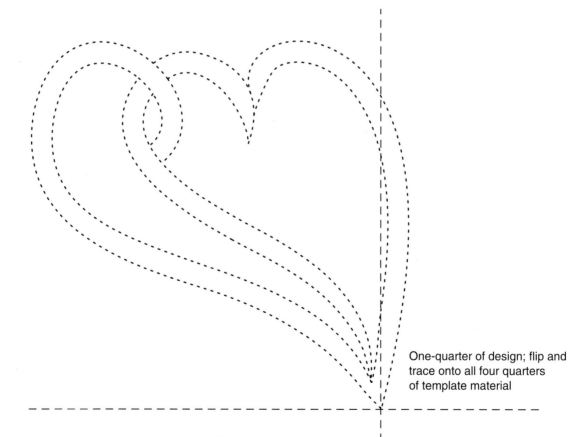

One-quarter of design; flip and
trace onto all four quarters
of template material

**Intertwined Heart Quilting Design
for Plain Squares**

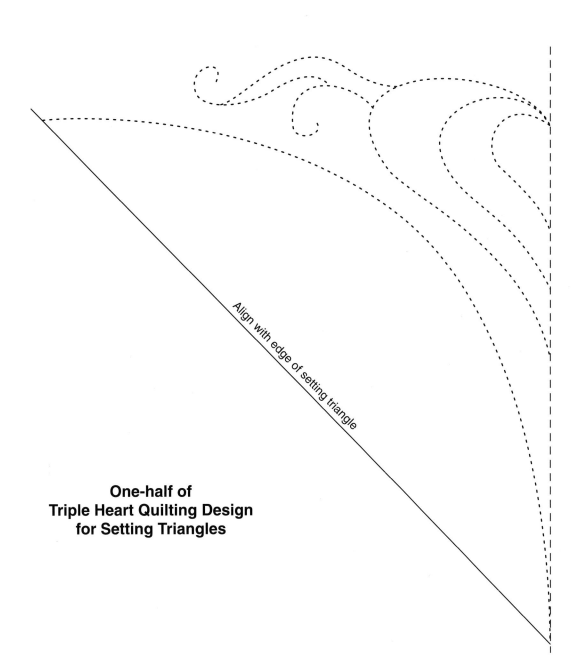

Align with edge of setting triangle

**One-half of
Triple Heart Quilting Design
for Setting Triangles**

Pineapple Askew

Quiltmaker: Nancy Ota

The twenty-first century is officially here! Quiltmakers are calling on modern technology like never before to experiment with favorite traditional block designs. With the assistance of a computer, Nancy has created a dramatic, asymmetrical look in her bursting-with-color Pineapple quilt.

Skill Level: Challenging

Size: Finished quilt is 59½ inches square
Finished block is 7 inches square

Fabrics and Supplies

This quilt takes advantage of an unusual off-the-bolt multicolored print in the blocks and narrow borders. This print contains areas of yellow, orange, blue, green, and rose that blend and flow together. The way the quiltmaker cut it gives the illusion that many fabrics are used throughout the blocks. If you are unable to locate this type of fabric, you can easily substitute hand-dyed or other commercial prints to achieve a similar appearance in your quilt.

✓ 4¼ yards of chocolate brown swirly print fabric for the blocks and borders

✓ 1¾ yards of a multicolored, blended print fabric for the blocks and narrow border

✓ 1½ yards of blue/violet mottled print fabric for the blocks

✓ ½ yard of deep brown/black print fabric for the binding

✓ ½ yard of dark purple solid fabric for the blocks

✓ 3¾ yards of fabric for the quilt back

✓ Twin-size quilt batting (72 × 90 inches)

✓ Rotary cutter, ruler, and mat

✓ Approximately 60 sheets of 8½ × 11-inch tracing paper

Cutting

Instructions are for quick cutting all of the block pieces and border strips with a rotary cutter and ruler. These measurements include ¼-inch seam allowances. Measurements for the border strips are longer than needed; trim them to the exact length when adding them to the quilt top. The blocks are made from strips cut in two different widths. However, to make the cutting process easier, all of the strips are cut to the same 1¾-inch width. Paper piecing allows you to trim strips to the correct length and width as you add them to the paper foundations. The number of

strips listed is only approximate because of the unusual type of multicolored print fabric used. The yardages are generous enough so that you can cut a few additional strips if you wish to include more pieces of a particular color in your own quilt.

From the chocolate brown swirly print fabric, cut:
- One 42 × 63-inch length. Cut this length into four 5½ × 63-inch strips for the outer borders and four 1½ × 63-inch strips for the inner borders.
- One 42 × 90-inch length. Cut this length into fifty-one 1¾ × 42-inch strips for the blocks.

From the multicolored print fabric, cut:
- Four ¾ × 63-inch strips for the narrow borders
- Three 2¼ × 39-inch crosswise strips for the blocks. These strips will be cut into 2¼-inch squares after the desired color placement is determined.
- Twenty-two 1¾ × 39-inch crosswise strips for the blocks

From the blue/violet mottled print fabric, cut:
- Twenty-eight 1¾ × 42-inch strips for the blocks

From the deep brown/black print fabric, cut:
- Six 2½ × 42-inch strips for the binding

From the dark purple solid fabric, cut:
- Eight 1¾ × 42-inch strips for the blocks

Color Placement in the Pineapple Blocks

There are basically just two different fabric arrangements needed for the 36 blocks in this quilt, as shown in **Block Diagram 1** and **Block Diagram 2** on page 114. The numbered piecing sequence is indicated on each block diagram, and it is the same for each block. However, each block highlights a different color from the multicolored print fabric, so for easy reference, see the "Featured Color Chart" on page 114, which lists the number of Block 1s and Block 2s to make in each of the featured colors. Refer to this chart often as you piece the 7-inch blocks. It will also be useful when piecing the border units.

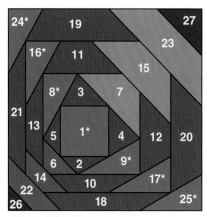

*Featured color

Block 1 Diagram

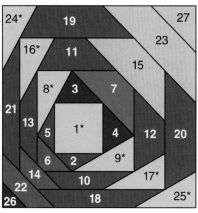

*Featured color

Block 2 Diagram

FEATURED COLOR CHART

Make the indicated number of blocks or units using the following colors in the featured color positions. The block diagrams indicate clearly where to place these featured colors.

Number of Blocks	Featured Color
Block 1	
14	Blue-green
10	Yellow-green
5	Yellow-orange
1	Red-orange
1	Red
1	Red-violet
Block 2	
3	Yellow-green
1	Blue-green
Border Unit	
7	Blue-green
3	Yellow-green
1	Yellow-orange
1	Red-orange
Border Unit Reversed	
8	Blue-green
2	Yellow-green
1	Yellow-orange
1	Red

Preparing the Paper Foundations

This quilt consists of thirty-six 7-inch blocks, 12 border units, 12 border units reversed, and four small border corner blocks, each of which is pieced on a tracing paper foundation.

1. To make the tracing paper foundations for the 7-inch blocks, start by making five photocopies of the 7-inch Pineapple Block Foundation Pattern on page 120, checking to make sure that they are 100 percent accurate in size.

2. Layer eight sheets of tracing paper underneath one of the photocopies and staple all of the edges together to hold them securely in place.

3. With a short to medium stitch length and no thread on top or in the bobbin of your sewing machine, stitch over the lines of the photocopied block foundation pattern. This will perforate all of the tracing paper at once, creating eight identical paper foundations. Repeat this process with the remaining four photocopied foundation patterns to make a total of 40 tracing paper foundations.

4. In the same manner, make tracing paper foundations for the 12 border units and for the 12 border units reversed, using the full-size Border Unit Foundation Pattern and Border Unit Reversed Foundation Pattern shown on page 119.

5. In the same manner, make tracing paper foundations for the four small border corner blocks, using the full-size Border Corner Block Foundation Pattern shown on page 118.

PHOTOCOPIES AND HOT IRONS DON'T MIX!

From using photocopied paper foundations to piece quilts, Nancy Ota discovered that the bottom of her iron sometimes became stained and that smudged areas were also beginning to appear on some of her fabrics. Her son, Chris, helped her discover the reason. Photocopies actually consist of minute particles of plastic, which are transferred to the paper during the photocopying process. If a heated iron is placed over a photocopied image, it can easily melt those tiny bits of plastic onto both itself and a piece of fabric. Nancy's solution is to place an accurately sized photocopy of a quilt block over several layers of tracing paper. She then stitches over the photocopy with an unthreaded sewing machine, perforating the sewing lines of the quilt block. Then she discards the photocopy and uses only the perforated tracing paper foundations for paper piecing her quilts.

Piecing the Pineapple Blocks

The 36 asymmetrical blocks in this quilt are pieced from the center square outward, in the numerical sequence shown in the **Block 1 Diagram** and **Block 2 Diagram.**

1. For Block 1, check the "Featured Color Chart" and select the featured color for each block. Start by cutting a 2¼-inch square of the appropriate color from the 2¼-inch strip of multicolored print fabric.

2. Referring to the block diagram for the piecing sequence, place a featured print center square right side up over square 1 on the tracing paper foundation. Center the square so that its ¼-inch seam allowances extend beyond the perforated lines. Pin the featured color center square on the side of the paper foundation you will be sewing on.

3. Referring to **Block 1 Diagram,** place a 1¾-inch chocolate brown strip right sides together along one side of the center square, aligning the edges. Insert a pin at each end to help in aligning the strip with the center square. Check to make sure that this strip is straight, that it covers all the necessary lines, and that there is ample seam allowance. Pin the strip in place. You may wish to trim it to a manageable length, remembering to allow for the ¼-inch seam allowances needed.

4. Adjust your sewing machine to 14 to 18 stitches per inch. Flip the paper foundation so the fabric side is facing down and the plain paper side is facing up. Stitch along the line between piece 1 and 2. Start sewing a bit before the fabric and sew directly on tracing paper seam line to a point beyond the edge of the fabric.

5. Make sure that the strip is sewn straight and then trim the seam allowance to ¼ inch. Open the strip and finger press it flat.

6. Trim the unsewn edge of the chocolate brown strip at the angles indicated by the lines on the tracing paper foundation, making sure to allow ¼-inch seam allowances.

7. In the same manner, referring to the piecing sequence in **Block 1 Diagram,** add a chocolate brown strip in positions 3, 4, and 5.

8. Continue to construct the block by adding appropriately colored strips, referring to the piecing sequence in **Block 1 Diagram.** Continue to finger press the seams flat and trim the strips, allowing for the ¼-inch seam allowances as needed.

FOUNDATIONS WITH EXTRA GRIP

Use the underside of the needle-punched tracing paper foundation as the side to which you pin fabrics. This is the side where the sewing machine needle comes out as it "stitches" through the tracing paper to perforate the seam lines. These tiny holes will be slightly raised or bumpy on the underside, and this texture can help hold fabrics in place as you foundation piece.

9. Make a total of 32 Block 1s, referring to the "Featured Color Chart" on page 114 as needed. Do not remove the tracing paper foundations from the blocks at this time.

10. In the same manner, make four Block 2s, referring to the "Featured Color Chart" on page 114 and **Block 2 Diagram** on page 114 for correct color placements. Do not remove the tracing paper foundations at this time.

Assembling the Quilt Top

1. Referring to the **Quilt Diagram** and the quilt photograph on page 112, place the 36 blocks in six horizontal rows of six blocks each.

2. Sew the blocks together into rows, pinning generously to match seams and corners. Press the seams open to reduce the bulk, if desired. Do not remove the tracing paper foundations at this time.

3. Sew the six rows of blocks together, pressing the seam allowances in alternate directions, or open if desired, to reduce bulk.

Piecing the Border Units

There are 24 pieced border units and four corner squares that complete the quilt top. They are pieced on tracing paper foundations in the same manner as the 7-inch blocks were.

R = Border unit reversed

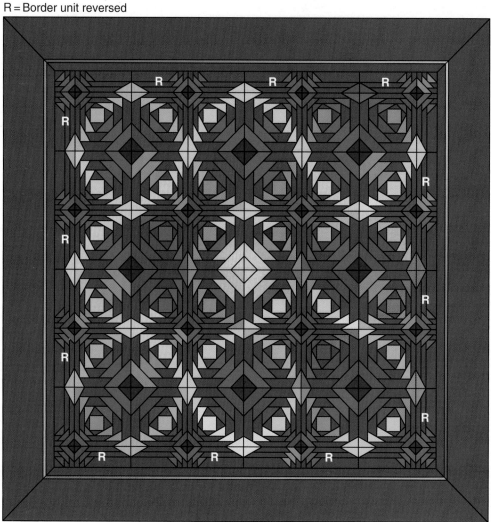

Quilt Diagram

Referring to the **Border Unit Diagram** for color placement and the numbered piecing sequence, piece the border units. The "Featured Color Chart" on page 114 indicates how many border units to make in each featured color. Finger press and trim the seam allowances as you sew. Make a total of 12 border units and 12 border units reversed. Do not remove the tracing paper foundations at this time.

*Featured color

Border Unit

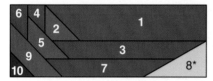

Border Unit Reversed

Border Unit Diagram

Piecing Border Corner Squares

Referring to the **Border Corner Block Diagram** for color placement and the piecing sequence, make four border corner blocks. Do not remove the tracing paper foundations at this time.

Border Corner Block Diagram

Attaching the Pieced Borders to the Quilt Top

1. Referring to the **Quilt Diagram** for color placement, sew six border units together to make the pieced border for each side of the quilt top.

2. Lay out a pieced border at the top and bottom edge of each side of the quilt top.

3. Sew the top and bottom pieced borders to the quilt top, pinning carefully to match seams. Press the seam allowances toward the top edge of the quilt.

4. Sew a border corner block to each end of the remaining two border strips. Place a strip at each side edge of the quilt top.

5. Sew the side borders to the quilt top, pinning carefully to match seams. Press the seam allowances toward the border strips.

Assembling and Attaching the Outer Borders

1. To make the outer borders, refer to the **Quilt Diagram** and sew together a $1\frac{1}{2} \times 63$-inch brown border strip, a $\frac{3}{4} \times 63$-inch multicolored border strip, and a $5\frac{1}{2} \times 63$-inch chocolate brown border strip. Press all of the seam allowances away from the multicolored strip. Make four outer border units.

2. Crease the midpoint of each outer border unit and place a pin at the midpoint on each side of the quilt top. Referring to the **Quilt Diagram,** sew the borders to the quilt top, beginning and ending each seam $\frac{1}{4}$ inch from the edge of the quilt top and mitering the corner seams. Press the corner seams open and trim the excess fabric. For more information on mitering, see page 160.

Quilting and Finishing

1. Carefully remove all of the tracing paper foundations. Starting with the center square of each block, use a seam ripper to gently loosen the tracing paper. Tweezers are also helpful for removing paper foundations.

2. Mark quilting designs as desired. The quilt shown is quilted in an overall pattern that runs through the center of each block, as indicated in the **Quilting Diagram** on page 118.

3. Divide the backing fabric into two equal $1\frac{7}{8}$-yard lengths and remove the selvages. Sew the two pieces of fabric together along the long edges and press this seam open.

4. Layer the quilt back, batting, and quilt top. The seam in the quilt back should be centered under the quilt top. Baste; then trim the quilt back and batting to approximately 3 inches larger than the quilt top on all sides.

5. Quilt all marked designs, adding any additional quilting as desired.

6. From the 2½ × 42-inch dark brown strips, make approximately 250 inches of double-fold, straight-grain binding. See page 164 for information on making and attaching binding.

7. Sew the binding to the quilt top. Trim the excess backing and batting. Hand-sew the folded edge of the binding to the back of the quilt.

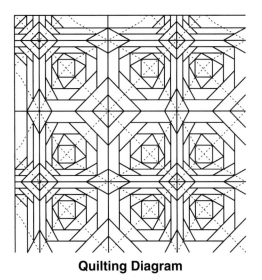

Quilting Diagram

Border Corner Block Foundation Pattern

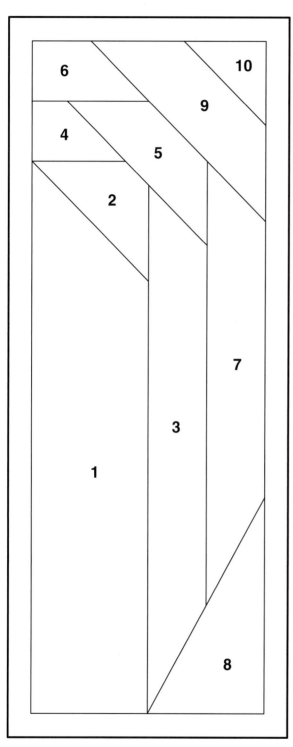

Border Unit Foundation Pattern

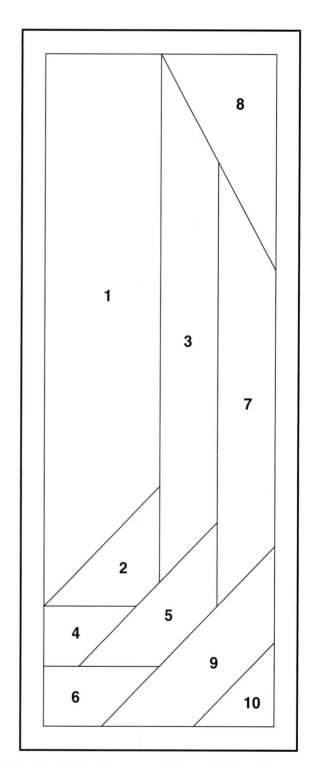

Border Unit Reversed Foundation Pattern

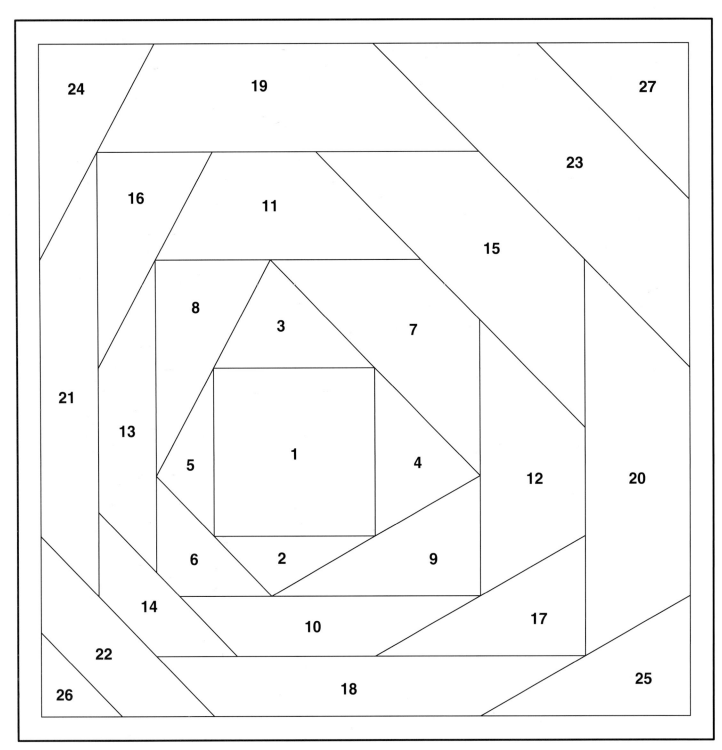

Pineapple Block Foundation Pattern

Twist and Shout

Quiltmaker: Sue Nickels

Could there be a more ideal project for using up those seemingly "unusable" scraps, snippets, strips, and strings? Sue's freewheeling wall quilt simply swirls with motion, and her brilliant color scheme crackles with excitement. Multicolored floss ties add still another element of fun.

Skill Level: Easy

Size: Finished quilt is 52½ inches square
Finished block is 8½ inches square

Fabrics and Supplies

- ✓ 1½ yards of black striped fabric for the outer border
- ✓ 1 yard of black solid fabric for the blocks, appliquéd vine, and binding
- ✓ ¾ yard of white "spotty" print fabric for the borders and corner squares
- ✓ ¼ yard of black multicolored, small-scale floral print for the blocks and corner squares
- ✓ ¼ yard of black "spotty" print fabric for the blocks
- ✓ ¼ yard of bright fuchsia print fabric for the narrow border
- ✓ One 3-inch-square scrap of bright orange check fabric for the corner squares
- ✓ Scraps *totaling* approximately 1½ yards in a wide variety of colors, values, and textures for the leaves, string-pieced blocks, and borders. You'll need lots and lots of bits and pieces, strips and strings, but not much of any single fabric.
- ✓ 3¼ yards of fabric for the quilt back
- ✓ Twin-size batting (72 × 90 inches)
- ✓ Rotary cutter, ruler, and mat
- ✓ Template material
- ✓ Freezer paper
- ✓ A few yards each of orange, bright yellow, fuchsia, and purple embroidery floss
- ✓ A large-eyed, sharp needle

Cutting

Make templates for the leaf appliqué patterns Leaf 1 through Leaf 4 on page 127. Appliqué pattern pieces are finished size; add the seam allowances when cutting them out of the fabric. Instructions for the string-pieced squares and borders are written for using freezer paper foundations. Measurements for the borders are longer than needed; trim them

to the exact length when they are added to the quilt top. Cut pieces in the following sequence:

From the black striped fabric, cut:
- Four 5½ × 54-inch strips for the outer borders

From the black solid fabric, cut:
- ½ yard for the binding; set this yardage aside.
- One 18-inch square for the bias vine
- Four 5⅛-inch squares. Cut each square in half diagonally to make 8 A triangles.

From the white spotty print, cut:
- Four 5½ × 27-inch strips for the borders
- Four 5½-inch B corner squares

From the black multicolored print, cut:
- One 5⅛ × 42-inch strip. Cut this strip into six 5⅛-inch squares; cut these squares in half diagonally to make 12 A triangles.
- Four 3-inch C corner squares

From the black spotty fabric, cut:
- One 5⅛ × 42-inch strip. Cut this strip into eight 5⅛-inch squares; cut these squares in half diagonally to make 16 A triangles.

From the fuchsia print, cut:
- Four 1½ × 42-inch strips for the inner borders

From the scrap of orange plaid fabric, cut:
- Four 1½-inch D corner squares

From the wide assortment of scraps in your scrap bag, cut:
- A total of 113 leaf appliqués, cutting a random number of pieces from templates Leaf 1 through Leaf 4

BEING LIVELY WITH LEFTOVERS

Leftover scraps from all of the print fabrics can be used for the appliquéd leaves and string-pieced squares and borders. Although some of the leaves may need to be cut from larger scraps, even the tiniest pieces of fabric will work well for string piecing the blocks and borders.

Making the String-Pieced Squares

String piecing is a technique by which you actually create your own fabric. Using freezer paper as a foundation makes it simple to work with scraps—even tiny "strings" of fabric. And cutting the blocks and borders to the correct sizes later is quick and easy with a rotary cutter and ruler.

1. Using a rotary cutter and ruler, cut two 3½ × 65-inch freezer paper foundations. These foundations will later be cut into 36 string-pieced blocks.

2. Position two strips or scraps of fabric right sides together on the matte side of one of the freezer paper foundations, as shown in **Diagram 1.** Using a ¼-inch seam allowance, sew the fabrics together through the freezer paper foundation, as shown. Open up the fabric and finger press the seam flat.

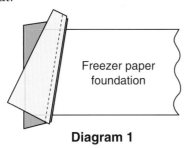

Freezer paper foundation

Diagram 1

3. Continue adding scraps of fabric to the freezer paper foundation, as shown in **Diagram 2,** finger pressing each seam flat before adding another piece of fabric. Take advantage of varying widths and angles of your own scraps for an interesting, free-form look. If your scraps are especially large or wide, trim them down a bit. Take care to cover the entire width and length of the freezer paper foundation as you work, to avoid gaps. Repeat Steps 1 through 3 to string piece another 3½ × 65-inch freezer paper foundation with fabric scraps.

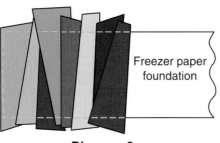

Freezer paper foundation

Diagram 2

4. Trim the edges of the fabric scraps even with the edges of the 3½-inch-wide freezer paper foundation, as shown in **Diagram 3.**

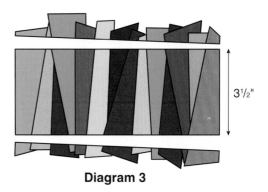

3½"

Diagram 3

5. Using a rotary cutter, cut this strip into 36 string-pieced 3½-inch squares and remove the freezer paper foundation from the wrong side of each square.

REMOVING THE FREEZER PAPER

To remove the freezer paper from the wrong side of the string-pieced squares and borders in this quilt, try this technique. Working from the freezer paper side, simply pinch each seam allowance between your thumb and index finger with the same kind of motion you'd use to separate one postage stamp from another. This helps to separate the freezer paper from the seams and makes it much easier to insert your thumbnail (or the blunt end of a seam ripper) and peel the freezer paper right out.

Making the String-Pieced Borders

1. Using a rotary cutter and ruler, cut four 3 × 38-inch freezer paper foundations.

2. Following the string-piecing procedure as described for the string-pieced squares, cover each of these foundations with fabric scraps.

3. In the same manner, use a rotary cutter to trim the fabrics even with the edges of the 3-inch-wide freezer paper foundations.

Piecing the Blocks

This quilt is composed of nine blocks, each containing four string-pieced squares and four A triangles. The blocks are identical, except for the color placement of the A triangles. Refer to the **Block Diagram** while piecing each block.

1. Sew two string-pieced squares together, pressing the seam allowances in opposite directions. Repeat for the other two squares, as shown in **Diagram 4.**

2. Sew the pairs of squares together, matching the center seam and pressing the seam allowance to one side. Make nine of these string-pieced squares, as shown in **Diagram 5.**

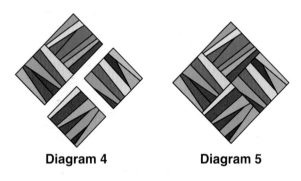

Diagram 4   **Diagram 5**

3. For Block Combination 1, sew a black solid A triangle to opposite edges of the string-pieced unit, as shown in **Diagram 6.** Press the seam allowances toward the A triangles. Complete the block by sewing a black solid A triangle to the remaining two edges. Press the seam allowances toward the A triangles. Make one block in this combination.

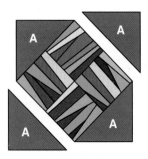

Diagram 6

4. For Block Combination 2, refer to the **Block Diagram** and follow the same procedure, substituting a black spotty A triangle for each black solid A. Make four blocks in this combination.

5. For Block Combination 3, refer to the **Block Diagram** and follow the same piecing procedure, substituting three black floral A triangles and one black solid A triangle to complete the block. Make four blocks in this combination.

Block Combination 1
Make 1

Block Combination 2
Make 4

Block Combination 3
Make 4

Block Diagram

Assembling the Quilt Top

1. Referring to the **Quilt Diagram** for block placement, lay out the nine blocks in three rows of three blocks each.

2. Sew the nine blocks together in rows of three blocks each, pressing the seam allowances in opposite directions between the rows.

3. Sew the three rows of blocks together, pressing the seam allowances toward the top edge of the quilt top.

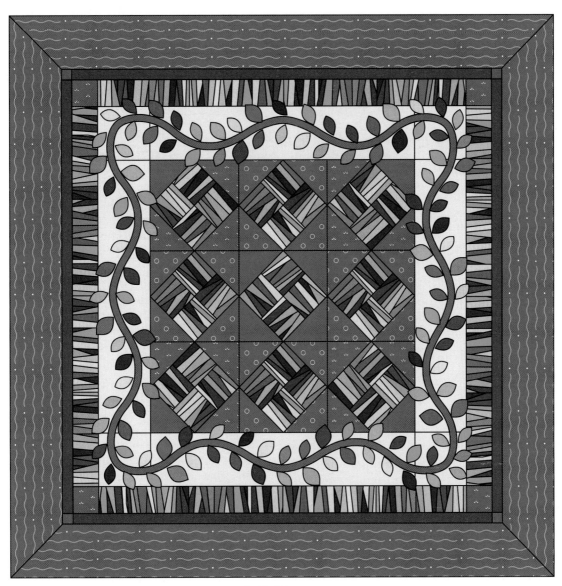

Quilt Diagram

Preparing the Appliqué Vines and Leaves

The quilt shown is appliquéd completely by machine; choose the method of appliqué you prefer.

1. For instructions on making continuous bias, refer to page 165. Use the 18-inch square of black solid fabric to cut a 144-inch continuous bias strip approximately 1⅜ inches wide. Refer to page 158 for tips on using bias presser bars to make perfectly finished vines. Finish the 144-inch-long bias vine to a width of approximately ½ inch.

2. If you choose hand appliqué, refer to page 157 for more information. Prepare the 113 leaf appliqués according to whatever appliqué method you choose.

Adding and Appliquéing the Borders

1. Measure the quilt top both vertically and horizontally. Because the quilt is square, these measurements should be the same. Trim each of the 5½ × 27-inch white spotty print border strips to this measurement.

2. Referring to the **Quilt Diagram** on page 125, sew a trimmed white spotty border strip to the left and right sides of the quilt top. Press the seam allowances toward the border strips.

3. Sew a white spotty B square to each end of the remaining two trimmed border strips. Press the seam allowances away from the B squares. Sew one of these strips to the top and one to the bottom edges of the quilt top, referring to the **Quilt Diagram.** Press the seam allowances toward the border strips.

4. Position the bias vine on the white border, as shown in the **Quilt Diagram.** The vine will be slightly longer than needed; trim it as necessary. Pin or baste the vine in place and stitch it down, using your preferred method of appliqué.

5. Measure the quilt top again and trim each of the string-pieced border strips to this new measurement.

6. Sew a trimmed string-pieced border strip to the left and the right sides of the quilt top. Press the seam allowances away from the string-pieced borders.

7. Sew a black print C square to each end of the remaining two string-pieced border strips. Press the seam allowances toward the C squares. Sew one of these strips to the top and one to the bottom edge of the quilt top, as shown in the **Quilt Diagram.** Press the seam allowances away from the string-pieced border strips.

8. Position the leaf appliqués along the vine, referring to the **Quilt Diagram.** Place approximately 28 leaves on each side, varying their sizes and allowing some of the leaves to overlap the quilt top and the string-pieced borders. Pin or baste each leaf in position and stitch with your preferred method of appliqué.

9. Measure the quilt top with the string-pieced border added and trim the $1\frac{1}{2} \times 42$-inch fuchsia border strips to this new measurement.

10. Sew a trimmed fuchsia border strip to the left and the right sides of the quilt top. Press the seam allowances toward the fuchsia border strips.

11. Sew an orange D corner square to each end of the remaining two fuchsia border strips and press the seam allowances toward the D squares. Sew one of these strips to the top and one to the bottom edge of the quilt top, as shown in the **Quilt Diagram** on page 125. Press the seam allowances toward the fucshia border strips.

12. Sew a $5\frac{1}{2} \times 54$-inch black striped border strip to each side of the quilt top, mitering the corner seams. Refer to page 160 for instructions on mitering border seams.

Quilting and Finishing

1. Mark quilting designs as desired. The quilt shown is quilted in the ditch around all of the string-pieced squares, around the appliquéd vines and leaves, and in the ditch between each of the border strips. The A triangles are quilted with free-form feathered vines. The outer black borders are also quilted with feathered vines, as indicated in the **Border Quilting Diagram.** If you wish to do the same type of quilting in the outer borders of your quilt, start by marking a vine that flows in the curves you desire. Use the Feather Motif to mark feathered shapes along the vines. To space the feathers evenly, work from the outer corners inward, so that any necessary adjustments can be made gradually as you approach the center of each border. If you wish to quilt free-form feathered vines in the A triangles, follow the same process for creating curved vines and adding feathered shapes in those areas.

Border Quilting Diagram

2. Divide the backing fabric into two equal $58\frac{1}{2}$-inch pieces. Remove the selvages and sew the pieces together along the long edges. This seam will run parallel to the sides of the quilt. Press the seam allowances open.

3. Layer the quilt back, batting, and quilt top. Position the quilt back so that seam is centered under the quilt top. Baste; then trim the quilt back and batting so that they are approximately 3 inches larger than the quilt top on all sides.

4. Quilt all marked designs, adding additional quilting as desired. The quilt shown was quilted entirely by machine; you may choose to quilt by hand or machine.

5. From the reserved ½ yard of black fabric, make approximately 220 inches of double-fold bias binding. Refer to page 164 for instructions on making and attaching binding.

6. Sew the binding to the quilt top. Trim the excess backing and batting, and use matching thread and an invisible stitch to hand-sew the folded edge of the binding to the back of the quilt.

7. Thread a large-eyed, sharp needle with two strands each of yellow, orange, fuchsia and purple embroidery floss. From the front side of the quilt, insert the threaded needle into the center of each block, referring to the **Quilt Diagram** on page 125. Leave a tail of approximately 3 inches and bring the needle back up to the top of the quilt. Trim the floss even with the first 3-inch tail. Tie the two tails in a square knot and trim the ends to approximately 1 inch. Repeat the process three times in each of the string-pieced borders.

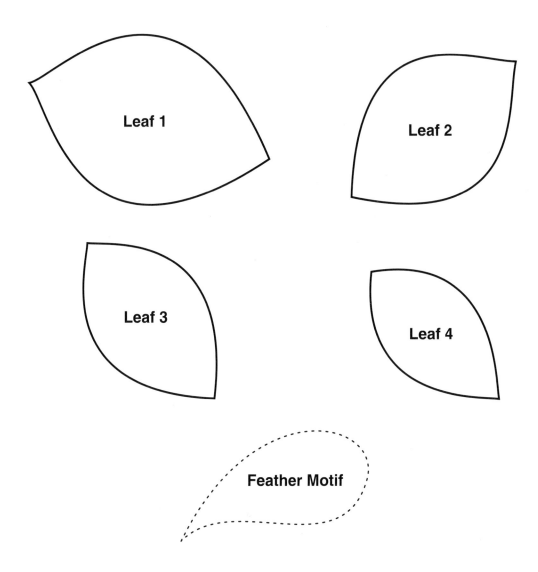

Leaf 1

Leaf 2

Leaf 3

Leaf 4

Feather Motif

Gemstones

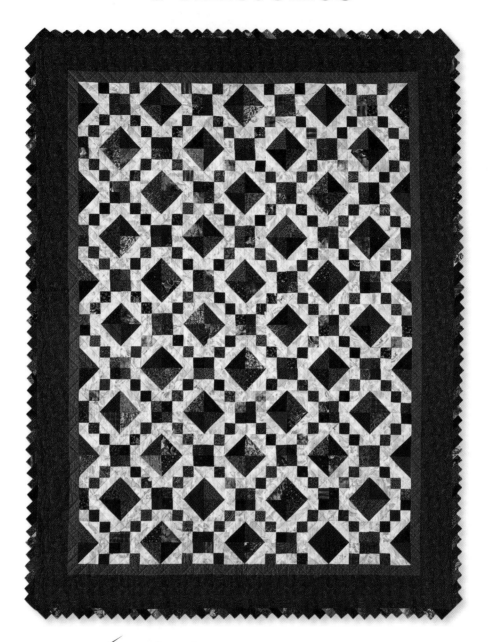

Quiltmaker: Jeanne Jenzano

Jeanne's prairie point edging works well on this quilt, playing off the many angles and diagonal lines within the design. To prove that looks can be deceiving, just one easy-to-piece block made of squares and triangles repeats to create this active and interesting pattern. Rich jewel-tone fabrics and a multifaceted design combine to create a dazzling quilt.

Skill Level: Easy

Size: Finished quilt is approximately 80 × 104 inches, not including the prairie point edging
Finished block is 8 inches square

Fabrics and Supplies

- ✓ 3½ yards of light print fabric for patch-work
- ✓ 3½ yards total of assorted medium and dark jewel-tone print fabrics for patch-work (You should have a minimum of ¼ yard per print.)
- ✓ ¾ yard of teal print fabric for inner border
- ✓ 2 yards of purple print fabric for outer border
- ✓ 3½ yards total of assorted medium and dark jewel-tone print fabrics for prairie point edging, or ¾ yard of fabric for binding
- ✓ 7½ yards of fabric for quilt back
- ✓ Queen-size quilt batting (90 × 108 inches)
- ✓ Rotary cutter, ruler, and mat
- ✓ Template plastic (optional)

Cutting

All measurements include ¼-inch seam allowances. The measurements for the borders include several extra inches in length; trim them to the exact length before sewing them to the quilt top. The instructions are written for quick-cutting the pieces using a rotary cutter and ruler. Cut all strips across the fabric. Note that for some of the pieces, the quick-cutting method will result in left-over strips of fabric.

You may want to cut just enough pieces to make one block to test your cutting and seam allowances for accuracy. If your finished block does not measure the size stated above, you can make adjustments before cutting all your fabric.

From the light print fabric, cut:
- Twenty-two 2½-inch strips for strip sets.

- 176 triangles: Cut eleven 4⅞-inch strips. From these strips cut 88 squares, each 4⅞ inches square. Cut each square in half diagonally to make two triangles.

From the medium and dark print fabrics, cut:
- Twenty-two 2½-inch strips for strip sets.
- 176 triangles: Cut eleven 4⅞-inch strips. From these strips cut 88 squares, each 4⅞ inches square. Cut each square in half diagonally to make two triangles.

From the teal print fabric, cut:
- Nine 2½-inch border strips

From the purple print fabric, cut:
- Nine 6½-inch border strips

From the fabrics for the prairie points, cut:
- Twenty-three 5-inch strips. From these strips cut 182 squares, each 5 inches square.

Fabric Key

☐ Light print

☐ Medium and dark prints

☐ Purple print

■ Teal print

Piecing the Blocks

1. Referring to the **Fabric Key** and **Strip Set Diagram,** make 22 strip sets by sewing together pairs of 2½-inch-wide light and medium or dark strips. Press seam allowances toward the darker strips.

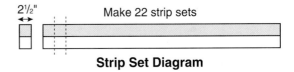

2½" Make 22 strip sets

Strip Set Diagram

2. From the strip sets, cut 352 segments, each 2½ inches wide.

3. Join pairs of segments to form Four-Patch units as shown in **Diagram 1**. Press seam allowances to one side. Make 176 Four-Patch units.

4. Join a light triangle to a dark triangle along the long edges to form a Triangle-Square, as shown in **Diagram 2**. Press the seam allowance toward the dark triangle. Make 176 Triangle-Square units.

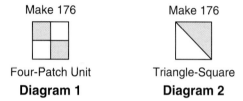

Make 176   Make 176

Four-Patch Unit   Triangle-Square

Diagram 1   **Diagram 2**

5. To piece one block, lay out two Triangle-Square units and two Four-Patch units as shown in the **Block Assembly Diagram.** Pay careful attention to the placement of light and dark fabrics within the block.

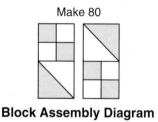

Make 80

Block Assembly Diagram

6. Join units in two rows. Press seam allowances toward the Triangle-Square units. Join the rows. Press the seam allowance to one side. The block should measure 8½ inches square, including seam allowances.

7. Make 80 blocks. You will have extra Triangle-Squares and Four-Patch units to use for the top and bottom rows of the quilt top.

Assembling the Quilt Top

1. Referring to the **Quilt Diagram** and the photo on page 128, lay out the blocks in ten horizontal rows with eight blocks in each row. Note that the blocks are not all set in the same position. The positions alternate as shown in **Diagram 3**. Check to be sure all blocks are positioned so the light-colored pieces create a secondary design as shown. The heavy lines on the **Quilt Diagram** indicate the rows of blocks.

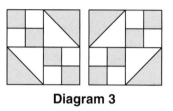

Diagram 3

2. Lay out the extra Triangle-Square and Four-Patch units to make a narrower row for the top and bottom edges of the quilt, as shown in **Diagram 4**. You will use eight Triangle-Squares and eight Four-Patch units for each row.

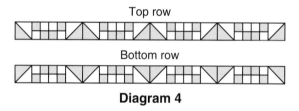

Top row

Bottom row

Diagram 4

3. Join the units in the top and bottom rows. Join the rest of the blocks in horizontal rows. Press the seam allowances in alternate directions from row to row.

4. Sew the rows together. Press the seam allowances to one side. The quilt top should measure 64½ × 88½ inches, including seam allowances.

5. For the top and bottom borders, join two teal border strips for each border. For the side borders, cut one teal border strip in half, then join two and one half border strips for each side border.

6. Measure the quilt from top to bottom through the center and trim the side borders to the correct length. Sew borders to the sides of the quilt top. Press the seam allowances toward the borders.

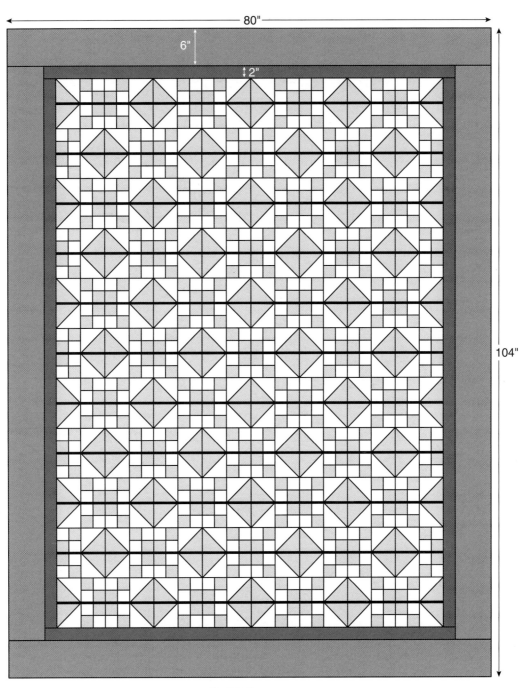

Quilt Diagram

7. Measure the width of the quilt, including the side borders, through the center. Trim the top and bottom borders to this measurement. Sew borders to the top and bottom ends of the quilt top. Press the seam allowances toward the borders.

8. Piece the outer borders from the purple print fabric and sew them to the quilt top in the same manner as you did for the inner border.

Quilting and Finishing

1. If you plan to finish the edges of your quilt with prairie points, prepare them and stitch them to the quilt top before layering and basting. See "Prairie Point Pizzazz" on the opposite page for details on making and attaching prairie points.

2. Mark desired quilting designs onto the quilt top. The quilting design used on the borders of the quilt shown is provided on this page. If you are finishing the outer edges of the quilt with prairie points, leave at least ½ inch unquilted along the outer edge.

3. To piece the quilt back, divide the backing fabric into three 2½-yard pieces. Join the three panels; press the seam allowances toward the outer panels. The seams will run parallel to the top and bottom edges of the quilt.

4. Layer the quilt back, batting, and quilt top; baste. Trim the quilt back and batting so they are approximately 3 inches larger than the quilt top on all sides.

5. Quilt all marked designs, and add additional quilting as desired.

6. If you prefer to finish the quilt edges with binding, make approximately 380 inches of double-fold binding. See page 164 for suggested binding widths and instructions on making and attaching binding. Sew the binding to the quilt. Trim the excess batting and backing, and hand-sew the folded edge of the binding to the back of the quilt.

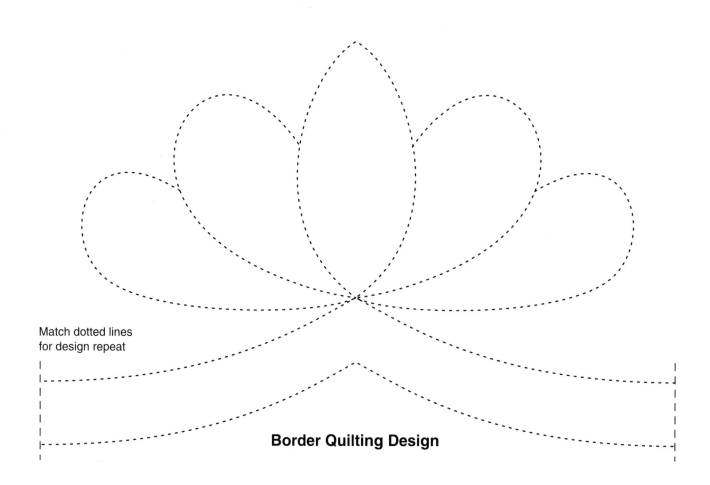

Match dotted lines for design repeat

Border Quilting Design

PRAIRIE POINT PIZZAZZ

1. For this quilt, you will need 182 squares, each 5 inches square. Fold each square in half diagonally with wrong sides together. Then fold it in half again, as shown in **Diagram 1**, to create the finished prairie point triangle.

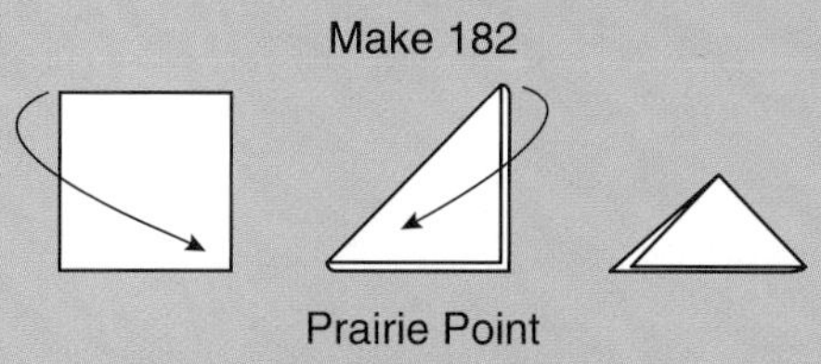

Make 182

Prairie Point
Diagram 1

points on each of the side edges. You will need to adjust the spacing of prairie points on each side to make sure the points meet in the corners. Stitch the prairie points to the quilt top with a ¼-inch seam.

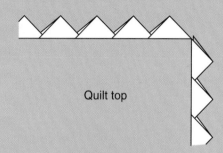

Quilt top

Diagram 2

2. To finish the edge of your quilt with prairie points, position the triangles so that the folds all face in the same direction. Slip the folded edge of each prairie point into the open edge of the prairie point next to it, as shown in **Diagram 2**, and pin or baste the prairie points to your quilt. The long edges of the triangles should be even with the raw edges of the quilt top. The quilt pictured has 37 prairie points on the top and bottom edges and 54 prairie

3. After the quilting is finished, trim the backing and batting even with the edges of the quilt top. Then trim away an additional ¼ inch from the batting edges only to reduce bulk. Turn the triangles away from the quilt so the seam allowance is folded toward the wrong side of the quilt. Fold the backing and batting under a ¼ inch and pin them to the quilt so they cover the bottom edges of the prairie points. Blindstitch the backing in place to finish your quilt.

Tessellating Sea Horses

Quiltmaker: Donna Radner

Sea horses frolic through an underwater fantasyland
in this clever variation of the familiar Log Cabin.
Inspired by *Log Cabin in the Round Designs* by Barbara
Schaffeld and Bev Vickery, Donna has created the illusion
of curves in her quilt without a single curved seam. Her
results are dramatic, yet you'll be surprised at how simple
this technique really is.

Skill Level: Intermediate

Size: Finished quilt is 95 × 100 inches
Finished block is 5 inches square

Fabrics and Supplies

While many traditional florals and small-scale prints will mix well with the "underwater" theme of this quilt, combine them with lots of large-scale florals and exotic prints, abstracts, batiks, and other unusual prints, too.

- ✓ Scraps *totaling* approximately 4½ yards of a wide variety of light pink, blue, and teal prints for the blocks
- ✓ Scraps *totaling* approximately 4½ yards of a wide variety of medium and dark blues and teals for the blocks and borders
- ✓ Scraps *totaling* approximately 3½ yards of a wide variety of medium and dark fuchsias and purples for the blocks and borders
- ✓ ½ yard *each* of a dark blue fabric and a teal print fabric for the binding
- ✓ 9 yards of fabric for the quilt back
- ✓ King-size batting (120 inches square)
- ✓ Rotary cutter, ruler, and mat

Cutting

Instructions are for quick cutting the blocks, border strips, and binding with a rotary cutter and ruler. All measurements include ¼-inch seam allowances. To speed the cutting process, the fabrics may be layered before cutting them into strips. The strips may then be cut into the necessary number of segments.

From one of the blue or teal prints, cut:
- One 18-inch square for continuous strip bias binding. The balance of this fabric may be cut into strips for the blocks and borders.

From the light pink, blue, and teal prints, cut:
- Three hundred eighteen 1 × 1½-inch B strips
- Two hundred ten 1 × 2½-inch E strips
- Two hundred ten 1 × 3-inch F strips
- One hundred eight 1 × 4-inch I strips
- Two hundred ten 1 × 4½-inch J strips
- One hundred eight 1½ × 2-inch M strips
- One hundred eight 1½ × 2½-inch D strips
- One hundred eight 1½ × 3½-inch O strips
- One hundred eight 1½ × 4-inch H strips
- One hundred eight 1½ × 5-inch Q strips

From the medium and dark blue and teal prints, cut:
- One hundred eighty-six 1 × 1-inch A squares
- Sixty-four 1 × 2-inch N strips
- Sixty-four 1 × 2½-inch E strips
- Sixty-four 1 × 3½-inch P strips
- One hundred twenty-six 1 × 4-inch I strips
- Sixty-four 1 × 5-inch R strips
- Sixty-four 1 × 5½-inch S strips
- One hundred twenty-six 1½ × 1½-inch C squares
- One hundred twenty-six 1½ × 2½-inch D strips
- One hundred twenty-six 1½ × 3-inch G strips
- One hundred twenty-six 1½ × 4-inch H strips
- One hundred twenty-six 1½ × 4½-inch K strips
- One hundred twenty-six 1½ × 5½-inch L strips

From the fuchsia and purple prints, cut:
- One hundred twenty-eight 1 × 1-inch A squares
- Eighty-four 1 × 2½-inch E strips
- Forty-four 1 × 2-inch N strips
- Forty-four 1 × 3½-inch P strips
- Eighty-four 1 × 4-inch I strips
- Forty-four 1 × 5-inch R strips
- Eighty-four 1½ × 1½-inch C squares
- Eighty-four 1½ × 2½-inch D strips
- Eighty-four 1½ × 3-inch G strips
- Eighty-four 1½ × 4-inch H strips
- Eighty-four 1½ × 4½-inch K strips
- Eighty-four 1½ × 5½-inch L strips

From the remaining medium and dark blue, teal, fuchsia, and purple prints, cut:
- 1½-inch wide strips in varying lengths, to total approximately 1,700 inches, for piecing the borders

- Eight 1½-inch C squares
- Eight 1½ × 2½-inch D strips
- Eight 1½ × 3½-inch O strips
- Eight 1½ × 4½-inch K strips
- Four 1½ × 5½-inch strips L strips

Piecing the Blocks

This quilt contains 318 Log Cabin blocks in four different color variations. The illusion of curves is created by using strips in two different widths within the same block.

Sew the blocks together in the same way you would assemble any Log Cabin–style block, referring to the block diagrams as you work on each of the variations. Press all seam allowances toward the last strip added.

Piecing Block 1

Block 1 is made up of medium and dark blue and teal prints combined with light pink, blue, and teal prints.

1. Sew a dark A square to a light A square, as shown in **Diagram 1.** The dark A square will be the center of the block. Sew a light B strip to this A/A unit, trimming the B strip to match the length of the A unit, if necessary.

Diagram 1

2. Sew a dark C square to the A/A/B unit, as shown in **Diagram 2.**

Diagram 2

3. Referring to the **Block 1 Diagram,** continue adding strips, working clockwise, in the following order: a dark D strip, a light E strip, a light F strip, a dark G strip, a dark H strip, a light I strip, a light J strip, a dark K strip, and a dark L strip.

4. Make 126 of Block 1.

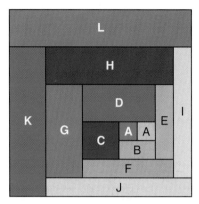

Block 1 Diagram

Piecing Block 2

Block 2 is also made up of medium and dark blue and teal prints combined with light pink, blue, and teal prints.

1. Sew a dark A square to a light B strip, as shown in **Diagram 3.** The dark A square will be the center of Block 2. Add a light M strip, followed by a dark N strip, as shown.

Diagram 3

2. Referring to the **Block 2 Diagram,** continue constructing Block 2 in the same manner as for Block 1, working clockwise as you add the remaining strips in the following order: a dark E strip, a light D strip, a light O strip, a dark P strip, a dark I strip, a light H strip, a light Q strip, a dark R strip, and a dark S strip. Make 64 of Block 2.

Piecing Block 3

Block 3 is made up of medium and dark fuchsia and purple prints combined with light pink, blue, and teal prints. Referring to the **Block 3 Diagram,** follow the same piecing process as for Block 1, substituting a medium or dark fuchsia or purple for the medium/dark blue/teal. Make 84 of Block 3.

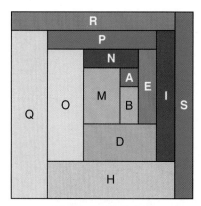

Block 2 Diagram

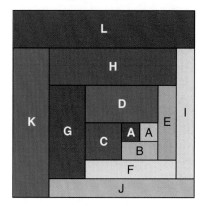

Block 3 Diagram

Piecing Block 4

Block 4 is also made up of medium and dark fuchsia and purple prints combined with light pink, blue, and teal prints. Referring to the **Block 4 Diagram,** follow the same piecing process as for Block 2, substituting a medium or dark fuchsia or purple for the medium/dark blue/teal. Make 44 of Block 4.

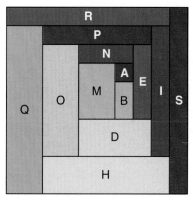

Block 4 Diagram

Assembling the Quilt Top

1. Referring to the **Quilt Diagram** on page 138 for block and color placement, lay out the Log Cabin blocks in 17 horizontal rows of 18 blocks each.

2. Sew the blocks together into 17 horizontal rows. Press the seam allowances in opposite directions between alternate rows.

3. Sew the rows of blocks together, pinning carefully to match seams. Press the seam allowances toward the top edge of the quilt top.

Piecing the Borders

1. Referring to **Diagram 4,** sew enough 1½-inch-wide strips together end to end, to create twenty 85½-inch randomly pieced lengths.

Diagram 4

2. Sew these randomly pieced lengths together to make four 5½ × 85½-inch lengths, as shown in **Diagram 5.** Two of these lengths will be used for the side borders.

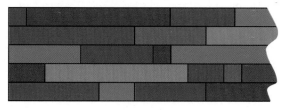

Diagram 5

3. Referring to **Diagram 5** and the **Quilt Diagram** on page 72, cut two 5½ × 40½-inch Y border units. Press the seam allowances to one side.

4. Referring to **Diagram 5** and the **Quilt Diagram,** cut two 5½ × 20½-inch Z border units. Press the seam allowances to one side.

5. Referring to the **Quilt Diagram** for block placement, complete the top border by sewing together a Z border unit, a Block 1, a Block 2, a Block 2, a Block 1, a Y border unit, a Block 1, and a Block 2, as shown. Press the seam allowances in the opposite direction from those in the top row of the quilt top.

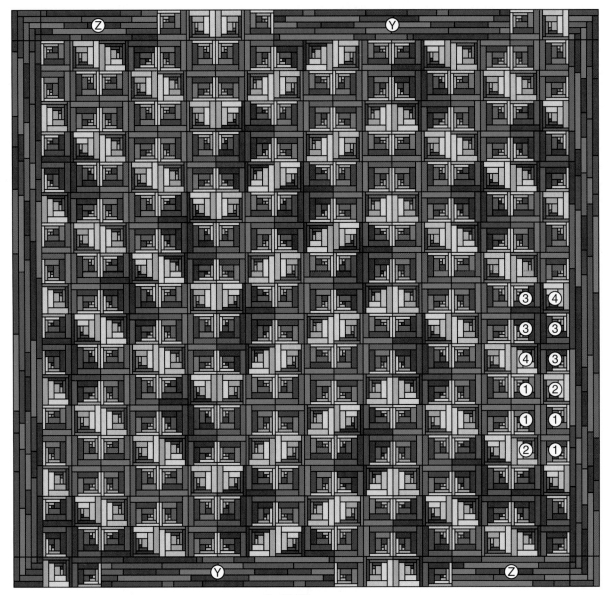

Quilt Diagram

6. Referring to the **Quilt Diagram** for block placement, complete the bottom border in the same manner, by sewing together a Block 4, a Block 3, a Y border unit, a Block 1, a Block 2, a Block 4, a Block 3, and a Z border unit. Press the seam allowances in the opposite direction from those in the bottom row of the quilt top.

Piecing the Corner Blocks

The corner blocks are made up of 1½-inch-wide strips. These strips may be medium or dark

blue, teal, purple, or fuchsia. There are no light fabrics in the corner blocks. As you select your fabrics for these blocks, take care to include some of the same ones that appear at the ends of each of the four border strips. By using some of the same fabrics in the corner blocks, the entire border will appear to be more unified and continuous.

1. Referring to the **Corner Block Diagram,** sew two C squares together, pressing the seam allowance toward the last piece added. Sew a D strip to the right side of the two C squares, followed by another D strip at the bottom edge of the C unit, as shown.

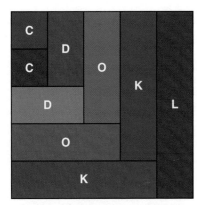

Corner Block Diagram

2. Referring to the **Corner Block Diagram,** continue constructing the block by adding an O strip to both the right and bottom edges.

3. Referring to the **Corner Block Diagram,** sew a K strip to both the right and bottom edges, as shown.

4. Sew an L strip to the right edge of the unit, completing the corner block.

5. Make four corner blocks.

Attaching the Borders to the Quilt Top

1. Referring to the **Quilt Diagram,** sew the top and bottom borders to the quilt top, taking care to align block seams where necessary. Press the seam allowances toward the edge of the quilt.

2. Referring to the **Quilt Diagram** for placement, sew a corner square at each end of the left and right border strips. Press the seam allowances away from the corner squares.

3. Sew left and right side borders to the proper side edges of the quilt top, making certain that they are positioned correctly. Press the seam allowances toward the outer edge of the quilt.

Quilting and Finishing

1. Mark quilting designs as desired. The quilt shown is quilted in an overall pattern that generally follows the curves in the pieced design. The **Quilting Diagram** indicates the quilting design.

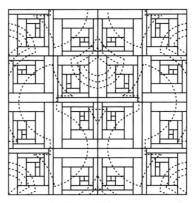

Quilting Diagram

2. Divide the backing fabric into three equal 108-inch-long pieces. Remove the selvages and sew the pieces together along the long edges, creating a three-panel quilt back. Press these seams open and place them so that they will lie parallel to the top and bottom of the quilt.

3. Layer the quilt back, batting, and quilt top. The backing fabric should extend equally beyond all edges of the quilt top, so that the quilt back is centered. Baste; then trim the quilt back to approximately 3 inches larger than the quilt top on all sides. Quilt all marked designs and add any additional quilting as desired.

4. From each of the binding fabrics, make approximately 200 inches of double-fold, continuous bias binding. Sew these two long strips together with a diagonal seam. For more information on making and attaching continuous bias binding, see page 164.

5. Sew the binding to the quilt top. Trim the excess backing and batting. Using matching thread and an invisible stitch, hand-sew the folded edge of the binding to the back of the quilt.

Princess Feather and Rose of Sharon

Quiltmaker: Dana Klein

Unusual color choices set this unique quilt apart from standard versions of this classic pattern. Four large Princess Feather blocks, with a central Rose of Sharon appliqué, work together beautifully. The stylized flower shapes and whimsical stars sprinkled in the border give the quilt an almost folk-art character.

Skill Level: Challenging

Size: Finished quilt is 82 inches square
Finished block is 33 inches square

Fabrics and Supplies

- ✓ 5½ yards of solid green fabric for appliqués, borders, and binding
- ✓ 5 yards of solid khaki fabric for blocks and border appliqués
- ✓ 1 yard of deep rose print fabric for appliqués and unfilled piping border
- ✓ ¼ yard of light pink print fabric for appliqués
- ✓ ¼ yard of solid yellow fabric for appliqués
- ✓ 2½ yards of 90-inch wide fabric for quilt back
- ✓ Queen-size quilt batting (90 × 108 inches)
- ✓ Rotary cutter, ruler, and mat
- ✓ Template plastic
- ✓ Thread to match the appliqué fabrics

Cutting

The cutting dimensions for borders include ¼-inch seam allowances for the widths and several extra inches in length; trim the borders to the exact length when they are added to the quilt top. The dimensions for the large background squares include an extra 1½ inches; trim the blocks to the correct size after the appliqué is complete. The patterns for the appliqués are given finished size on pages 144–147. Tips on making and using templates are on page 153. Add seam allowances when cutting the pieces from the fabric. Due to its size, the large feather appliqué pattern is given in two pieces; trace each piece and join them together as indicated.

From the solid green fabric, cut:
- Two 8½ × 86-inch top and bottom border strips and two 8½ × 70-inch side border strips
- 32 large feather appliqués
- 4 long bud stem appliqués
- 4 short bud stem appliqués
- 8 double-leaf units
- Reserve the remaining fabric for binding

From the solid khaki fabric, cut:
- Four 35-inch background squares
- 28 small border feather appliqués
- 24 border stars

From the deep rose print fabric, cut:
- Seven 1 × 44-inch strips
- 5 large flowers
- 8 bud tips

From the light pink print fabric, cut:
- 5 small flowers

From the solid yellow fabric, cut:
- 5 flower centers

Making the Princess Feather Blocks

1. Fold a 35-inch khaki square in half vertically, horizontally, and diagonally both ways, and press lightly to form positioning lines.

2. Referring to the **Feather Appliqué Placement Diagram**, appliqué the eight large feather pieces first. Refer to page 158 for instructions on needle-turn appliqué. Place the stem bases approximately 3 inches from the center of the block. Be sure to place the stems so that the raw ends will be covered by the large flower when it is added at the center. To help position the feather correctly, place the template you used to make the appliqué piece over the appliqué piece and align the placement guidelines on the template with the positioning lines you pressed into the background fabric. Use matching thread to stitch the appliqué. See "Trimming from Behind Appliqués" for tips on cutting away the background fabric after adding the appliqués.

Feather Appliqué Placement Diagram

TRIMMING FROM BEHIND APPLIQUÉS

Background fabric should be trimmed away from behind appliqué pieces when elements are stacked on top of one another, such as the flower appliqués in this Princess Feather and Rose of Sharon quilt. Trimming away the excess fabric will keep the quilt top from becoming thick and bulky. The background should also be trimmed away when quilting is planned on an appliqué piece, such as on the appliqué feathers. Quilting will be easier without an extra layer of fabric. And, if the fabric underneath is darker than the appliqué, trimming will prevent the background from showing through.

To trim, turn the block or quilt top wrong-side up and work from the back. Pinch the background or underlying fabric and gently separate it from the appliqué piece. Make a small cut in the background fabric and then insert the scissors in the hole. Cut a scant ¼ inch to the inside of the line of appliqué stitches, as shown in the **Trimming Diagram**.

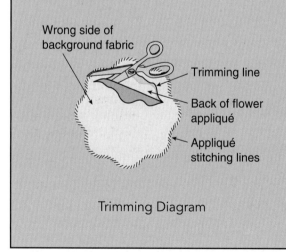

Wrong side of background fabric

Trimming line

Back of flower appliqué

Appliqué stitching lines

Trimming Diagram

Adding the Rose of Sharon

1. Sew together the four completed Princess Feather blocks in two rows of two blocks per row. Refer to page 159 for instructions on assembling quilt tops.

2. Referring to the photograph and the **Rose of Sharon Appliqué Placement Diagram** for accurate placement, position and appliqué the Rose of Sharon pieces in the center of the quilt. Use the seams that join the four blocks as positioning guidelines. Appliqué the pieces in this order: bud tips, leaf units, long stems, short stems, large flower, small flower, and flower center. The bud tips of the long stems are approximately 10 inches from the center of the quilt. The bud tips of the short stems are approximately 6 inches from the center.

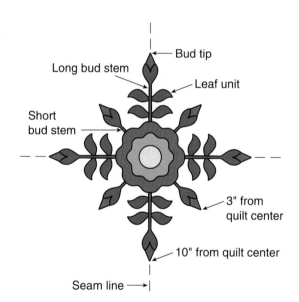

Bud tip

Long bud stem

Leaf unit

Short bud stem

3" from quilt center

10" from quilt center

Seam line →

Rose of Sharon Appliqué Placement Diagram

Appliquéing the Borders

These instructions are for appliquéing in the traditional manner. The borders on the quilt shown were actually reverse appliquéd. If you wish to try your hand at reverse appliqué, refer to "Reverse Appliqué for Border Motifs" on page 143.

1. Measure the inner quilt top. It should be approximately 66½ inches square, including seam allowances. Using your measurement, mark sewing

3. Center and appliqué the large flower so that it covers the ends of the stems. Add the small flower and then the flower center.

4. Measure and trim the completed blocks to 33½ inches square.

and cutting lines on the ends of the wrong side of the two 8½ × 70-inch side border strips. Wait to trim until after the appliqué is complete.

Add 16 inches to the measurement you just marked on the 70-inch side border strips, and mark sewing and cutting lines on the wrong side of the two 8½ × 86-inch top and bottom border strips. Wait to trim.

2. Referring to the photograph for placement, appliqué three pairs of small feathers and five stars to each side border. Appliqué four pairs of small feathers and seven stars to the top and bottom borders. Check the lengths of your com-

REVERSE APPLIQUÉ FOR BORDER MOTIFS

Reverse appliqué is a technique in which a top fabric is cut and turned back to reveal another fabric underneath. The feather motifs in the border of the Princess Feather and Rose of Sharon quilt can be treated as regular appliqués, or they can be worked in reverse appliqué as described here.

1. Make freezer paper patterns for the border feather and star.

2. Referring to the photograph for placement, position and press the templates onto the green border strips. Lightly mark placement lines along the edges of the patterns, then remove the patterns.

3. Use the patterns to cut out the khaki rectangles (for the feathers) and squares (for the stars). Make these 1 inch larger on all four sides than the appliqués.

4. Using a light box or window, position and pin the khaki fabric pieces beneath the marked placement lines, making sure there is adequate margin all the way around the lines. Carefully cut out the top fabric, cutting approximately ³⁄₁₆ inch *to the inside of the marked lines* and taking care not to cut into the underneath fabric.

5. Carefully clip concave curves and indentations. Use thread that matches the top fabric and an appliqué needle to turn under the raw edges and stitch in place.

pleted borders with the quilt top; trim off excess border strips along the marked cutting line.

Assembling the Quilt Top

1. To make the unfilled piping border that appears between the inner quilt and the appliquéd border, piece together the seven 1-inch-wide rose strips, joining them with straight seams. Press the seams open. Press the long strip in half lengthwise, with wrong sides together. Cut the pressed strip into four 68-inch lengths of piping.

2. Place a length of piping along one side of the quilt, aligning the raw edges of the piping with the raw edges of the quilt top, and pin in place.

3. Place a completed side border, right sides together, with the piping, and sew the border to the quilt, sewing in the piping at the same time. Press the seams toward the border. Trim the excess piping from the ends after sewing.

4. In the same manner, sew piping and a side border to the opposite side of the quilt top. Then add the remaining piping strips and borders to the top and bottom of the quilt top. The completed top should measure approximately 82½ inches square, including seam allowances.

Quilting and Finishing

1. Mark quilting designs. The quilting designs for the feathers and the star appliqués are printed within the appliqué patterns on pages 145–147. Refer to the photograph to determine the correct placement of the other quilting designs. The spaces at the ends of the long bud stem appliqués, the center of the four sides, and the inner corners of the quilt have additional feather designs. A 1-inch diagonal grid fills the rest of the inner quilt.

2. Layer the backing, batting, and quilt top; baste.

3. Quilt all marked designs. In addition to the quilting designs described above, the quilt shown has outline quilting in the ditch around all the appliqués. The border motifs are echo quilted.

4. Make double-fold binding from the remaining green fabric. You will need approximately 335 inches (9⅜ yards) of binding. Refer to page 164 for instructions on making and attaching binding. Sew the binding to the quilt.

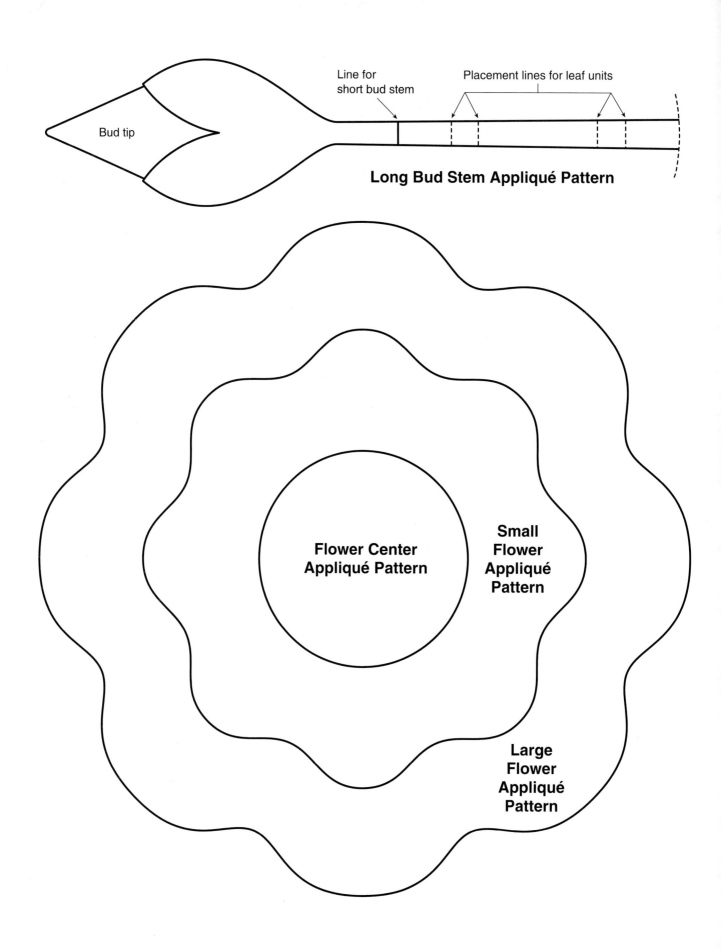

Bud tip

Line for
short bud stem

Placement lines for leaf units

Long Bud Stem Appliqué Pattern

**Flower Center
Appliqué Pattern**

**Small
Flower
Appliqué
Pattern**

**Large
Flower
Appliqué
Pattern**

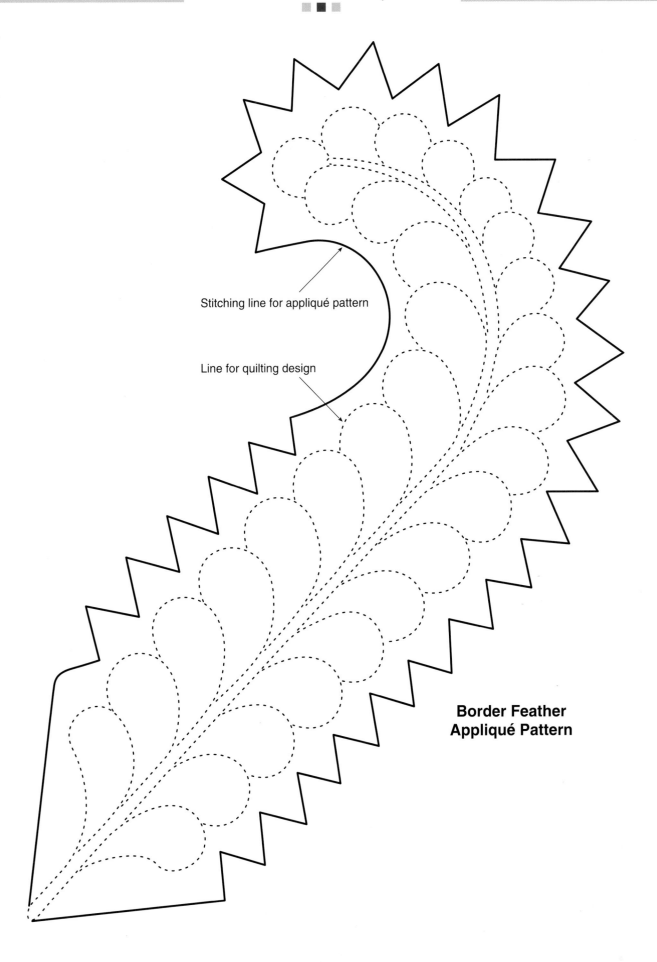

Stitching line for appliqué pattern

Line for quilting design

**Border Feather
Appliqué Pattern**

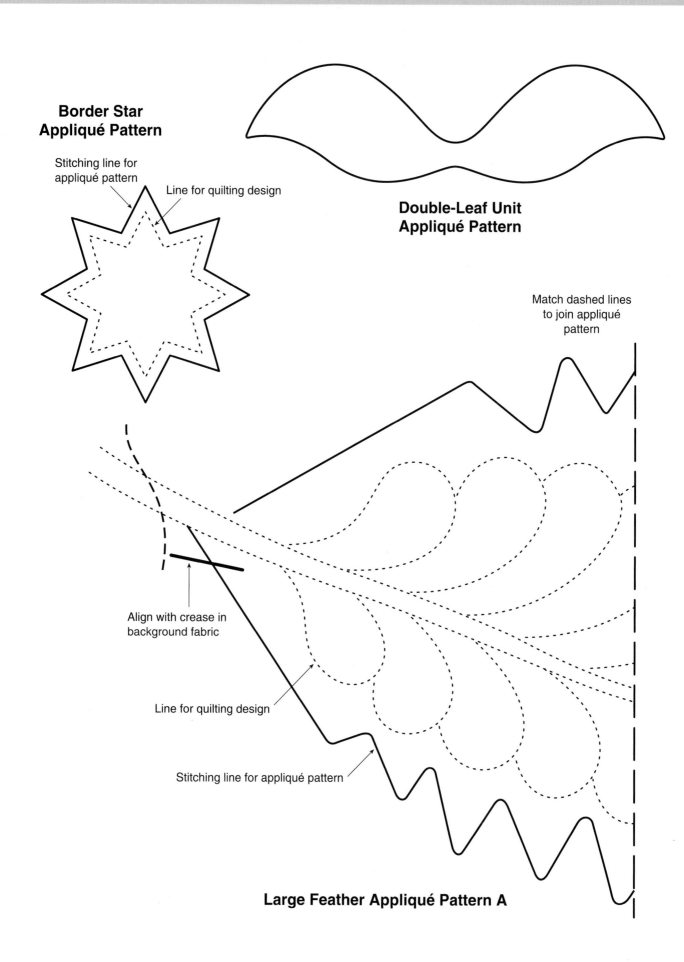

Border Star Appliqué Pattern

Stitching line for appliqué pattern

Line for quilting design

Double-Leaf Unit Appliqué Pattern

Match dashed lines to join appliqué pattern

Align with crease in background fabric

Line for quilting design

Stitching line for appliqué pattern

Large Feather Appliqué Pattern A

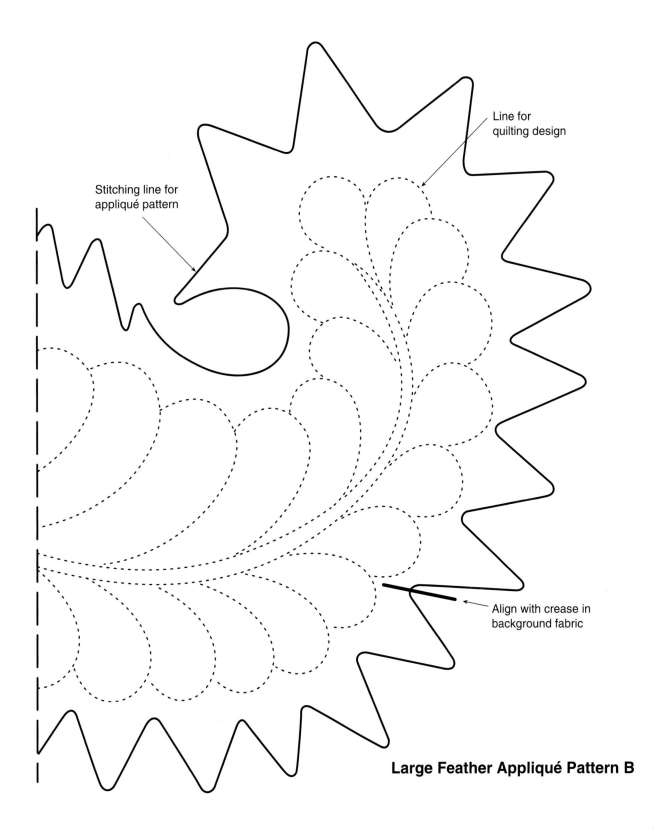

Line for
quilting design

Stitching line for
appliqué pattern

Align with crease in
background fabric

Large Feather Appliqué Pattern B

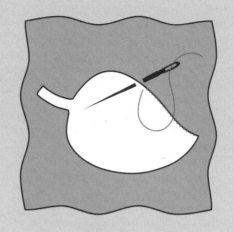

Tips & Techniques

■

Tips & Techniques

In this chapter you'll find detailed descriptions of general quiltmaking techniques as well as hints and tips designed to make your qluiltmaking successful and fun.

Supplies to Have on Hand

"Quiltmaking Basics" describes the supplies you'll need to get started on the projects in this book. "Quiltmaking Time-Savers" describes quilting tools that you may want to work with. A few of the projects also require specialized supplies; those supplies are listed with the projects.

Quiltmaking Basics

- **Needles.** Use *sharps* for hand sewing and appliqué and *betweens* for hand quilting. For both sharps and betweens, the larger the number, the smaller the needle. The general rule is to start with the larger-size needles and move to smaller ones as you gain experience. Experiment with different sizes to see which are most comfortable in your hand and the easiest to manipulate through the fabric.

- **Straight pins.** Do not use pins that have become burred or rusted; they may leave marks in your fabric. Long (1½-inch) pins with glass or plastic heads are easy to work with, especially when pinning layers.

- **Scissors.** If you are cutting your fabric with scissors, use a good, sharp pair of dressmaker's shears. Use these only on fabric. You should also have a pair of small, sharp embroidery scissors for trimming threads and seam allowances and a pair of general scissors for cutting paper and template plastic.

- **Iron and ironing board.** Careful pressing is important for accurate piecing. To save steps and increase efficiency, keep your ironing board and iron close to your sewing area.

- **Sewing machine.** Keep it clean, oiled, and in good working order.

- **Template plastic or cardboard.** Templates are rigid master patterns used to mark patchwork and appliqué shapes on fabric. Thin, semi-transparent plastic, available in sheets at quilt and craft shops, is ideal, although poster-weight cardboard can also be used for templates.

- **Thread.** Always use good-quality thread. For sewing, use either 100 percent cotton or cotton-covered polyester. For quilting, use special quilting thread.

Quiltmaking Time-Savers

- **Rotary cutter and cutting mat.** For greater speed and accuracy, you can cut all border strips and many other pieces with a rotary cutter instead of scissors. You must always use a specially designed cutting mat when working with a rotary cutter. The self-healing surface of the mat protects the work surface and helps to grip the fabric to keep it from slipping. An all-purpose cutting mat size is 18 × 24 inches. See the section on rotary cutting on page 152 for tips on using the cutter.

- **See-through ruler.** The companion to the rotary cutter and mat is the see-through plastic ruler. It comes in several sizes and shapes; a useful size to have on hand is a 6 × 24-inch heavy-duty ruler that is marked in inches, quarter inches, and eighth inches and has a 45 degree angle line for mitering. Also handy are a ruled plastic square, 12 × 12 inches or larger, and a 6 × 12-inch ruler for cutting segments from strip sets.

- **Plastic-coated freezer paper.** Quilters have discovered many handy uses for this type of paper, which is stocked in grocery stores with other food-wrapping supplies. Choose a quality brand, such as Reynolds.

About Fabric

Since fabric is the most essential element in a quilt, what you buy and how you treat it are important considerations. Buy the best that you can afford; you'll be far happier with the results if you work with good-quality materials. Read through this section for additional tips on selecting and preparing fabric.

Selecting Fabrics

The instructions for each of the quilts in this book include the amount of fabric you will need. When choosing falrics, most experienced quilters insist on 100 percent cotton broadcloth, or dress-weight, fabric. It presses well and handles easily, whether you are sewing by hand or machine.

If there is a quilt specialty shop in your area, the sales staff there can help you choose fabrics. Most home-sewing stores also have a section of all-cotton fabrics for quilters. If you have scraps left over from other sewing, use them only if they are all-cotton and all of similar weight.

CONSTRUCT A DESIGN WALL

There are several different ways to construct a design wall, using foam core board, white flannel, felt, fleece, or cotton batting. If you have the space to accommodate a design surface in your sewing room, start by purchasing a sheet of foam core board at any home improvement store. To cover a design wall that is 38 inches square or smaller, simply cut a length of 45-inch-wide white flannel approximately 3 inches larger than the board on all sides. Stretch the fabric tautly over the board, pulling the excess to the back side. Use thumbtacks or staples to secure the fabric on the back side of the board.

For versatility, a freestanding design wall is great. Just cover two large foam core boards using 72-inch white flannel and hinge them together. That way, it will be easy to fold and tuck the unit into a closet or slide under a bed for storage.

Gaining Color Confidence

Deciding on a color scheme and choosing the fabrics can seem daunting to a beginner. You can take some of the mystery out of the process by learning the basics of color theory. Consult books on color theory, or seek out a class at a local quilt shop or quilt conference. Learn how helpful a color wheel can be, and understand the importance of value (the lightness or darkness of a color) and scale (the size of the print). Your color confidence will grow as you learn the basics and then experiment with different combinations.

Purchasing Fabrics

The yardages given for projects in this book are based on 44- to 45-inch-wide fabrics. These yardages are adequate for both the template and rotary-cutting methods. They have been double-checked for accuracy and always include a little extra. Be aware, however, that fabric is sometimes narrower than the size listed on the bolt, and that any quilter, no matter how experienced, can make a mistake in cutting. It never hurts to buy an extra half-yard of the fabrics for your quilt, just to be safe.

Preparing Fabrics

For best results, prewash, dry, and press your fabrics before using them in your quilts.

Prewashing allows shrinkage to occur and removes finishes and sizing, softening the cloth and making it easier to handle. Washing also allows colors to bleed before light and dark fabrics are combined in a quilt. If one of your fabrics bleeds, set the dye by soaking the whole piece of fabric in a solution of three parts cold water to one part vinegar. Rinse the fabric two or three times in warm water. If the fabric still bleeds, don't use it in your quilt.

Keep in mind that prewashing might remove the lovely finish from chintz and polished cotton. If you want to use these fabrics to add sparkle to your quilts, save them for wallhangings or other items that won't need to be laundered.

To prewash, use your automatic washer, warm water, and a mild detergent. Dry fabric on a medium setting in your dryer or outdoors on a clothesline. It's a good idea to get in the habit of washing all your fabrics as soon as you bring them home, even if you're not planning to use them right away. Then, when you are ready to use a fabric, you won't have to wonder whether it's been washed.

While prewashing is best, some quilters prefer the crispness of unwashed fabric and feel they can achieve more accurate machine-sewn patchwork by using fabric right off the bolt. Some machine quilters like to use unwashed fabric, then wash the project after quilting and binding so the quilt looks crinkled and old-fashioned. The risk in washing after stitching is that colors may bleed.

FIND THE FADE FACTOR

To check your fabrics for fading, cut a small piece from each new print or solid you buy and tape the pieces to a window that gets lots of sun. After one week, compare the taped snippets of fabric to the original pieces to get a good idea of how quickly those fabrics might fade with continued exposure to sunlight.

Cutting the Fabric

For each project in this book, the cutting instructions follow the list of fabrics and supplies. Quilters who prefer the traditional method of making templates and scissor-cutting individual pieces will find full-size patterns or template sizes and cutting guidelines. For quilters who prefer to rotary cut, quick-cutting directions speed things along. You may want to try a combination of techniques, using scissors and templates for certain pattern pieces and the rotary cutter for straight pieces like the borders and bindings.

DUCT TAPE TO THE RESCUE

If you're cutting pieces of fabric that are longer than your cutting mat, consider borrowing a mat from a friend and taping it onto yours. Lay both mats face down and slide the edges together until they meet evenly. Join them together with a strip of duct tape and you'll be ready to turn the mats over and cut long strips of fabric easily.

For some of the projects there are no patterns. Other projects have foundation patterns for paper piecing. In these cases, you will either measure and cut squares, triangles, and rectangles directly from the fabric, or you will be instructed to cut and work with strips of fabric.

Although rotary cutting can be faster and more accurate than cutting with scissors, it does have one disadvantage: It does not always result in the most efficient use of fabric. In some cases, the quick-cutting method featured in the project will result in long strips of leftover fabric. Don't think of these as wasted bits of fabric; just add these strips to your scrap bag for future projects.

Tips on Rotary Cutting

- Keep the rotary cutter out of children's reach. The blade is extremely sharp!

- Make it a habit to slide the blade guard into place as soon as you stop cutting.

- Always cut *away* from yourself.

- Square off the end of your fabric before measuring and cutting pieces, as shown in **Diagram 1.** Place a ruled square or right-angle triangle on the fold, and place a 6 × 24-inch ruler against the side of the square. Hold the ruler in place, remove the square, and cut along the edge of the ruler. If you are left-handed, work from the other end of the fabric.

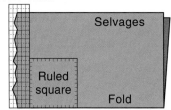

Diagram 1: *Square off the uneven edges of the fabric before cutting the strips.*

- Use the right cutter for the job. The large size is best for

cutting several layers. The small cutter is ideal for cutting around thick plastic templates since it is easier to control around curves and points.

- When cutting strips or rectangles, cut on the crosswise grain, as shown in **Diagram 2,** unless instructed otherwise. Strips can then be cut into squares, as shown. You can stack two or three folded strips on top of each other so you have four or six layers of fabric, and you will be cutting squares from all the strips at once.

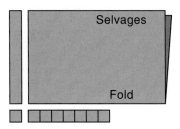

Diagram 2: *Cut strips or rectangles on the crosswise grain. Cut the strips into squares.*

- Check strips periodically to make sure the fabric is square and the strips are straight, not angled. (See **Diagram 3.**) If your strips are not straight, refold the fabric, making sure the selvages are even, square off the edge, and cut again.

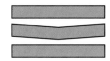

Diagram 3: *Check to see that the strips are straight. If they are angled, refold the fabric and square off the edge again.*

- Cut triangles from squares, as shown in **Diagram 4.** The project directions will tell you whether to cut the square into two triangles by making one diagonal cut (**Diagram 4A**) or into four triangles by making two diagonal cuts (**4B**).

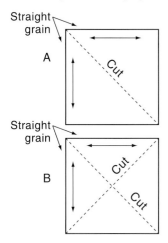

Diagram 4: Cut two triangles from a square by making one diagonal cut (A). Cut four triangles from a square by making two diagonal cuts (B).

Making and Using Templates

The patterns in this book are printed full size, with no drafting required. For some of the pieced projects, you will have the option of either making templates using the patterns or dimensions given and cutting fabric pieces individually, or using a rotary cutter to quick cut them.

Thin, semitransparent plastic makes excellent, durable templates. Lay the plastic over the book page, carefully trace the patterns onto the plastic, and cut them out with scissors. To make cardboard templates, transfer the patterns to tracing paper, glue the paper to the cardboard, and cut out the templates. Copy identification letters and any grain line instructions onto your templates. Always check your templates against the printed pattern for accuracy.

The patchwork patterns in the

TAPE YOUR RULERS

Even if the measurement line you need for cutting strips is actually on your rotary cutting ruler, it can be helpful to place a piece of masking tape on the underside of the ruler at whichever line you are using. The edge of the masking tape becomes an important visual guide that keeps you from having to look at all the other lines on the ruler each time you move it across the fabric.

book are printed with double lines: an inner dashed line and an outer solid line. If you intend to sew your patchwork by hand, trace the inner dashed line to make finished-size templates. Cut out the templates on the traced line. Draw around the template on the wrong side of the fabric, as shown in **Diagram 5**, leaving ½ inch between lines. The lines you draw are the sewing lines. Then mark the ¼-inch

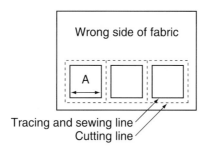

Diagram 5: If piecing by hand, mark around the template on the wrong side of the fabric. Cut it out, adding ¼-inch seam allowances on all sides.

seam allowances before you cut out the fabric pieces.

If you plan to sew your patchwork by machine, use the outer solid line and make your templates with seam allowances included. Draw around the templates on the wrong side of the fabric, as shown in **Diagram 6.** The line you draw is the cutting line. Sew with an exact ¼-inch seam for perfect patchwork.

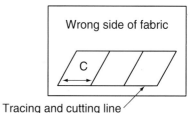

Diagram 6: If piecing by machine, use templates with seam allowances included.

Patterns for appliqué pieces are printed with only a single line. Make finished-size templates for appliqué pieces. Draw around templates on the right side of the fabric, as shown in **Diagram 7,** leaving ½ inch between pieces. The lines you draw will be your fold-under lines, or guides for turning under the edges of the appliqué pieces. Then add scant ¼-inch seam allowances as you cut out the pieces.

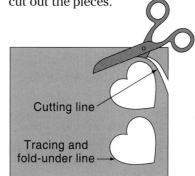

Diagram 7: Draw around the templates on the right side of the fabric for appliqué pieces. Add seam allowances as you cut out the pieces.

Tips on Piecing

The standard seam allowance for piecing is ¼ inch. For precise patchwork, where the pieces always meet exactly where they should, you must be vigilant about accurate seam allowances. Some sewing machines come with a handy seam allowance guide marked alongside the feed dogs. On other machines, the distance from the needle to the outside of the presser foot is ¼ inch. (Measure your machine to be sure this is accurate.) On machines that have no built-in guides, you can create your own. Measure ¼-inch from the needle and lay down a 2-inch-long piece of masking tape. Continue to add layers of masking tape on top of the first one until you have a raised edge against which you can guide fabric, automatically measuring the ¼-inch seam allowance.

When assembling pieced blocks, keep in mind these basic rules: Combine smaller pieces to make larger units, join larger units into rows or sections, and

join sections to complete the blocks. If you follow these rules, you should be able to build most blocks using only straight seams. Setting in pieces at an angle should only be done when necessary. (Pointers appear on the opposite page.)

Lay out the pieces for the block with right sides up, as shown in the project diagram, before you sew. For quilts with multiple blocks, cut out and piece a sample block first to make sure your fabrics work well together and you have cut out the pieces accurately.

Hand Piecing

For hand piecing, use finished-size templates to cut your fabric pieces. Join the pieces by matching marked sewing lines and securing them with pins. Sew with a running stitch from seam line to seam line, as shown in **Diagram 8,** rather than from raw edge to raw edge. As you sew, check to see that your stitching is staying on the lines, and make a backstitch every four or five stitches to reinforce and strengthen the seam. Secure the corners with an extra backstitch.

Diagram 8: Join the pieces with a running stitch, backstitching every four or five stitches.

When you cross a seam allowance of previously joined smaller units, leave the seam allowance free rather than stitching it down. Make a back-

stitch just before you cross, slip the needle through the seam allowance, make a backstitch after you cross, then resume stitching the seam. (See **Diagram 9.**) When your block is finished, press the seam allowances toward the darker fabrics.

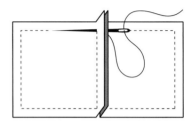

Diagram 9: When hand piecing, leave the seam allowances free by slipping through without stitching them down.

Machine Piecing

For machine piecing, cut the fabric pieces using templates with seam allowances included or use a rotary cutter to quick cut. Before sewing a block, sew a test seam to make sure you are taking accurate ¼-inch seams. Even ¹⁄₁₆ inch of inaccuracy can

GRADE SEAM ALLOWANCES

While it is usually recommended that seam allowances be pressed toward the darker fabric, sometimes the piecing order dictates pressing toward the lighter fabric instead. This can cause the edges of the darker seam allowance to "shadow through." If this happens, simply trim the darker seam allowance to a scant ¼ (or ³⁄₁₆) inch. At a full ¼ inch, the lighter seam allowance will then cover the raw edges of the darker fabric.

result in a block that is not the right size. Adjust your machine to sew 10 to 12 stitches per inch. Select a neutral-color thread such as a medium gray that blends well with the fabrics you are using.

Join the pieces by sewing from raw edge to raw edge. Press the seams before crossing them with other seans. Since the seam allowances will be stitched down when crossed with another seam, you'll need to think about the direction in which you want them to lie. Press the seam allowances toward darker fabrics whenever possible to prevent them from shadowing through lighter ones. For more information on pressing, see page 156.

When you join blocks into rows, press all the seam allowances in opposite directions from row to row. Then, when you join the rows, abut the pressed seam allowances to produce precise intersections.

In many quilts, you need to sew a large number of the same size or shape pieces together to create units for the blocks. For a bed-size quilt, this can mean a hundred or more squares, triangles, or rectangles that need to be stitched together. A time-saving method known as assembly-line piecing can reduce the drudgery. Run pairs of pieces

or units through the sewing machine one after another without cutting the thread, as shown in **Diagram 10.** Once all the units you need have been sewn, snip them apart and press. You can continue to add on more pieces to these units, assembly-line fashion, until the sections are the size you need.

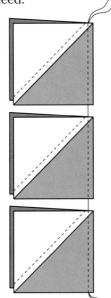

Diagram 10: *Feed the units through the machine without cutting the thread.*

Setting In Pieces

Not all patchwork patterns can be assembled with continuous straight seams. An example is the August quilt on page 40. Background pieces must be set

into the angled openings created by the diamonds. Setting in calls for precise stitching as you insert pieces into angles, as shown in **Diagram 11.** In this example, pieces A, B, and C are set in to the angles created by the four joined diamond pieces.

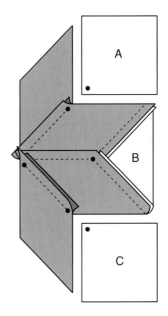

Diagram 11: *Setting-in calls for careful matching of points and precise stitching. Here, pieces A, B, and C are set into the angles created by the four joined diamonds.*

Setting In by Hand

Setting in by hand is simple. Follow the directions on page 153 to make finished-size templates. Trace the templates, then mark ¼-inch seam allowances before cutting out pieces.

1. Pin the piece to be set in to one side of the angle, right sides together, match corners exactly.

2. Starting ¼ inch from the outside edge and working to the corner, stitch along the marked seam line, as shown in **Diagram 12** on page 156, removing pins as you go. Stop ¼ inch from the inside corner, at your marked seam line. Knot the thread and clip it.

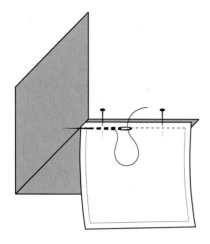

Diagram 12: Pin the pieces right sides together and stitch from the outside into the corner.

3. Bring the adjacent edge up and pin it to the other side of the angle, as shown in **Diagram 13.** Hand stitch the seam from the corner out, stopping ¼ inch from the edge at the end of the marked seam line.

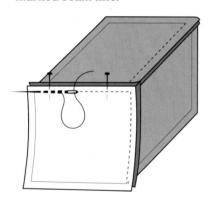

Diagram 13: Pin the adjacent edge to the other side of the angle and stitch from the corner to the outside.

Setting In by Machine

If you are setting in pieces by machine, make special templates that will allow you to mark dots on the fabric at the points where pieces will come together. By matching dots on the pattern pieces as they meet at the angle, you can be sure of a smooth fit.

To make these templates, first mark the sewing lines, then use a large needle to pierce a hole at each setting in point. (See **Diagram 14.**) As you trace the templates onto the wrong side of the fabric, push the tip of the pencil through each of these holes to create a dot. Mark all corners of each pattern piece. You may discover later that you want to turn the piece to adjust color or pattern placement; marking all the corners allows you that option.

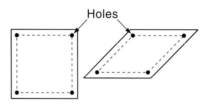

Diagram 14: For setting-in pieces by machine, make templates with holes at the setting-in points.

1. Pin a piece to one side of the angle with right sides together, matching the dots. Beginning and ending the seam with a backstitch, sew from the raw edge into the corner, and stop the stitching exactly on the marked corner dot. Don't allow any stitching to extend into the seam allowance. (See **Diagram 15.**)

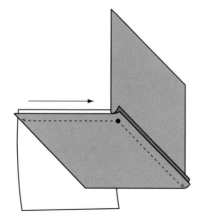

Diagram 15: Pin the piece to one side of the angle, matching dots. Stitch from the edge into the corner.

2. Remove the work from your machine to realign the pieces for the other side of the seam. Swing the other side of the angled piece up, match dots, and pin the pieces together.

3. Sew from the corner dot to the outside edge to complete the seam, again backstitching at the beginning and end. (See **Diagram 16.**) Press the seams toward the set-in piece.

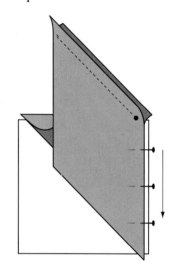

Diagram 16: Matching dots, pin the piece to the other side of the angle. Stitch from the corner dot to the outside edge.

Pressing Basics

Proper pressing can make a big difference in the appearance of a finished block or quilt top. Quilters are divided on the issue of whether a steam or dry iron is best. Experiment to see which works best for you. For each project, pressing instructions are given as needed in the step-by-step directions. Review the list of guidelines that follow to brush up on your general pressing techniques.

- Press a seam before crossing it with another seam.

- Press seam allowances to one side, not open.
- Press seams of adjacent rows of blocks, or rows within blocks, in opposite directions so the pressed seams will abut as the rows are joined. (See **Diagram 17.**)

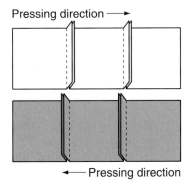

Diagram 17: *Press the seams of adjacent rows in opposite directions. When the rows are placed right sides together to be joined, the pressed seams will abut.*

LEATHER FINGERS

When you're pressing seams directionally, try wearing a leather thimble on the index finger of your left hand. The leather will protect your finger while you work with the placement of seam allowances and keep you from being burned by the iron.

- If possible, press seams toward darker fabrics to avoid show-through on the front of the quilt.
- Press, don't iron. Bring the iron down gently and firmly on the fabric; don't rub the iron over the patchwork.

- Avoid pressing appliqués on the right side after they have been stitched to the background fabric. They are prettiest when slightly puffed, rather than flat. To press appliqués, turn the piece over and press gently on the back of the background fabric.

Hand Appliqué

Several of the quilts in this book include beautiful appliqué. The true tests of fine appliqué work are smoothly turned, crisp edges and sharp points; no unsightly bumps or gaps; and nearly invisible stitches.

Depending on your personal preference, there are three popular techniques that can help you achieve flawless appliqué. Each of these methods is described in detail below.

For any of these methods, use thread that matches the appliqué pieces, and stitch the appliqués to the background fabric with a blind hem or appliqué stitch, as shown in **Diagram 18.** Invest in a package of long, thin size 11 or 12 needles marked sharps. Make stitches ⅛ inch apart or closer, and keep them snug.

When construchg appliqué

Diagram 18: *Stitch the appliqués to the background with a blind hem stitch. The stitches should be nearly invisible.*

blocks, always work from background to foreground. When an appliqué piece will be covered or overlapped by another, stitch the underneath piece to the background fabric first.

Basting-Back Method

1. Make finished-size cardboard or thin plastic templates. Mark around the templates on the right side of the fabric to draw fold-under lines. Draw lightly so the lines are thin.

2. Cut out the pieces a scant ¼ inch to the outside of the marked lines.

3. For each appliqué piece, turn the seam allowance under, folding along the marked line, and baste close to the fold with white or natural thread. Clip concave curves and clefts before basting. (See **Diagram 19.**) Do not baste back edges that will be covered by another appliqué.

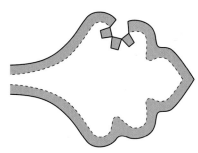

Diagram 19: *Clip any concave curves, then baste back the seam allowances.*

4. Pin the appliqués in place and stitch them to the background fabric. Remove the basting after the pieces are stitched down.

Freezer Paper Method

1. Make finished-size plastic templates for appliqué patterns.

2. Place templates on the smooth (not shiny) side of the freezer paper and draw around them. Do not add seam allowances. Cut out the patterns along the lines. Make a separate pattern for each appliqué piece.

3. Using a dry iron set on wool, press the paper patterns to the proper fabric, placing the shiny side of the paper on the right side of the fabric. Leave about ½ inch between pieces for seam allowances.

4. Cut out the appliqués ⅛ inch to the outside of the paper edge to allow for seams. Leave the paper attached to the fabric.

5. Pin the appliqué in place on the background fabric with the paper still attached. As you stitch the appliqué to the background, turn under the seam allowance along the edge of the freezer paper, aligning the fold of the fabric with the paper edge. Once the piece is stitched down completely, gently peel off the paper pattern.

Needle-Turn Method

1. Use plastic or cardboard templates to mark finished-size pieces. Mark lightly on the right side of the fabric.

2. Cut out the pieces a generous ⅛ inch larger than the finished size.

3. Pin the pieces in position on the background fabric. Use the tip and shank of your appliqué needle to turn under ½-inch-long sections of seam allowance at a time. As you turn under a section, press it flat with your thumb and then stitch it in place.

Making Bias Strips for Stems and Vines

Fabric strips cut on the bias have more give and are easier to manipulate than strips cut on

the straight grain. This makes them ideal for creating beautiful curving stems and vines and twisting ribbons. Bias strips enhance several of the projects in this book, including the Twist and Shout quilt on page 121. The quilt instructions include directions for cutting bias strips the proper width.

Cut bias strips with your rotary cutter using the 45 degree angle line on your see-through ruler. Straighten the left edge of your fabric as described on page 152. Align the 45 degree angle line on your see-through ruler with the bottom edge of the fabric, as shown in **Diagram 20A,** and cut along the edge of the ruler to trim off the corner. Move the ruler across the fabric, cutting parallel strips in the needed width, as shown in **20B.** Once the strips are cut, prepare them for appliqué by using a bias presser bar as described below.

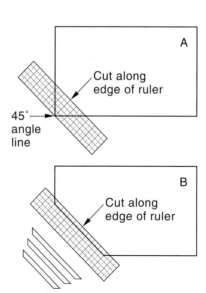

Diagram 20: *Use the 45 degree angle line on your see-through ruler to trim off the corner of the fabric (A). Then move the ruler across the fabric, cutting parallel strips of the width needed (B).*

Narrow bias strips for appliqué can be made using metal or plastic bars called bias presser bars or Celtic bars. You'll need this type of tool for making Twist and Shout on page 121, and August on page 40. Bias bars are available in quilt shops and through mail-order catalogs. The bar should be equal to the required finished width of the bias strip.

Cut a fabric strip wide enough to wrap around the bar and to allow for the ⅛-inch seam allowances. Fold the strip in half lengthwise, wrong sides facing, and using a ⅛-inch seam allowance, sew the long raw edges of the strip together. Insert the bar into the tube. Center the seam along the bar and press, as shown in **Diagram 21.** Continue to slide the bar along the tube, pressing as you go. Remove the bar and press the strip one more time.

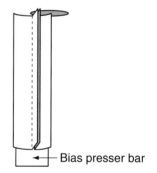

Bias presser bar

Diagram 21: *Slip bias presser bar into fabric tube. Center seam along top of bar and press.*

Machine Appliqué

Machine appliqué is ideal for decorative effects. It's a quick-and-easy way to add appliqué pieces to projects that you don't want to spend time hand stitching. Plus, machine appliqué stands up well to repeated washings, so it's great for place mats and clothing.

Satin stitch machine appliqué can be done on any sewing machine that has a zigzag stitch setting. Use a zigzag presser foot with a channel on the bottom that will allow the heavy ridge of stitching to feed evenly. Match your thread to the appliqué pieces. Set your machine for a medium-width zigzag stitch and a very short stitch length. Test stitch on a scrap of fabric. The stitches should form a band of color and be $\frac{1}{8}$ to $\frac{3}{16}$ inch wide. If necessary, loosen the top tension slightly so that the top thread is barely pulled to the wrong side.

1. To prepare the appliqué pieces, use Wonder-Under or a similar paper-backed fusible webbing, following the manufacturer's instructions. For most products, the procedure is the same: Trace the appliqué shapes onto the paper side of the webbing and roughly cut out the the designs, as shown in **Diagram 22.**

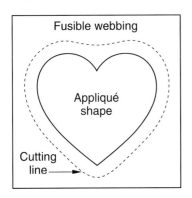

Diagram 22: Trace the appliqué shape onto the paper side of the webbing and roughly cut out the design.

2. Using a dry iron set on Wool, fuse the webbing onto the wrong side of the fabrics you have chosen for appliqués. Cut out the pieces along the tracing lines, as shown in **Diagram 23,** allowing

approximately ¼-inch underlap on adjacent pieces within a design. Peel off the paper backing, position the pieces on the background fabric, and fuse in place.

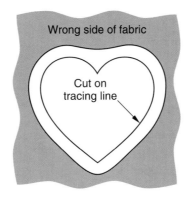

Diagram 23: Fuse the webbing onto the wrong side of the fabric and cut along the tracing line.

3. Stabilize the background fabric by pinning a sheet of typing paper or commercial stabilizer such as Tear-Away to the wrong side of the background fabric in the areas where you will be stitching. Some quilters like to use freezer paper as a stabilizer for machine appliqué.

4. Machine satin stitch around the edges of the appliqué pieces, covering the raw edges. Change thread colors to match the pieces. When stitching is complete, carefully tear away the stabilizer from the wrong side.

Assembling Quilt Tops

To assemble a quilt comprised of rows of blocks, such as Escargot in Plaid (page 95), refer to the quilt diagram or photograph and lay out all the pieced or appliqué blocks, plain blocks, and setting pieces right side up, positioned as they will be in the finished quilt.

Pin and sew all the blocks to-

gether in vertical or horizontal rows for straight-set quilts and in diagonal rows for diagonal-set quilts. Press the seams in opposite directions from row to row. Join the rows, abutting the pressed seam allowances so the intersections will be accurate.

To keep a large quilt top manageable, join rows into pairs first and then join the pairs, rather than add each row to an increasingly unwieldy top.

When pressing a completed top, press on the back first. Carefully clip and remove hang-ing threads, then press the front; be sure all the seams are flat.

PHOTOS POINT THE WAY

When deciding on a setting for a sampler quilt, start by laying out the blocks on a floor. That allows you to walk around the blocks and anaylze the balance of color in your arrangement from every angle and then decide how to balance the different types of blocks. Combine the blocks in several different ways, and take an instant film snapshot of each arrangement so you can compare them later and decide on a setting.

Tips for Successful Borders

For most of the quilts in this book, directions for adding the appropriate borders are included with the instructions for that quilt. Here are some general tips that can help you with any quilt you make.

- Cut borders to the desired finished width plus ½ inch for seam allowances. Always cut border strips several inches longer than needed, just to be safe. (Cutting instructions for borders in this book already include seam allowances and extra length.)

- Before adding borders, measure your completed inner quilt top. Measure through the center of the quilt rather than along the edges, which may have stretched from handling. Use this measurement to determine the exact length of your borders. This is an important step; if you don't measure first and simply give the edge of the quilt as much border as it "wants," you may end up with rippled edges on your quilt. Measuring and marking your borders first will allow you to make any necessary adjustment or ease in any fabric that may have stretched along the edge.

- Measure and mark sewing dimensions on the ends of borders before sewing them on, and wait to trim off excess fabric until after sewing.

- Fold border strips in half crosswise and press lightly or mark with a pin to indicate the halfway mark. Align this mark with the center point along the quilt side when pinning on the border.

- Press border seam allowances away from the center of the quilt.

Mitered Borders

Mitered borders add a professional touch to your quilt and are not hard to master if you keep in mind a few basics.

1. Start by measuring your finished quilt top through the center to determine the length the borders should be.

2. If you have multiple borders that are to be mitered, find and mark the center of each border strip. Match the centers, sew the strips together, and treat them as one unit.

3. With a ruler and pencil, mark a ¼-inch sewing line along one long edge of the border strip. For a multiple border, mark the inner strip that goes next to the quilt. Fold the strip in half crosswise and press lightly to mark the halfway point.

4. Starting at the halfway point, measure out in each direction to one-half of the desired finished border length, and make a mark on the sewing line.

5. Use a ruler that has a 45 degree angle line to mark the miter sewing line. Referring to **Diagram 24,** draw a line from the end mark made in Step 4 to the outer edge of the border strip. Mark a cutting line ¼ inch to the outside of the sewing line, but don't trim until after the border is sewn to the quilt top.

6. Pin the marked border strip to the quilt top, matching the crease at the halfway point to the center side of the quilt. Position the end marks on the border strip ¼ inch in from the raw edges of the quilt top. Pin the border to the quilt top, distributing any fullness evenly along the length of the border. Repeat for all remaining border strips.

7. Stitch the borders to the quilt top, starting and stopping at the end marks exactly ¼ inch from each end. Backstitch to secure the stitching. Press the seam allowances away from the quilt top.

8. Sew the miters by folding the quilt diagonally, right sides together, and aligning the marked miter lines on adjacent borders. Stitch from the inner corner mark all the way to the outer raw edge.

9. Check the accuracy of your miter, then trim the excess seam allowance.

Quilting Designs

Exquisite quilting is often the element that makes a quilt truly special. Even a simple quilt can be set apart by the fine workmanship demonstrated by small, even stitches. While some quilts lend themselves to very

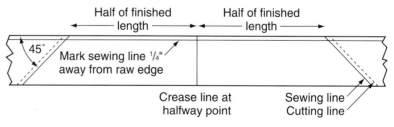

Diagram 24: Mark the border strips for mitering before sewing them to the quilt top.

simple quilting patterns, such as outline quilting, others are beautifully accented by cables, feathers, and floral designs. Suggestions for quilting designs are included with many of the project instructions. You can duplicate the design the quiltmaker used, create your own, or choose one of the many quilting templates available at quilt shops and through mail-order catalogs.

Some quilting needs no design template. Outline quilting simply follows them seams of the patchwork. It can be in the ditch, that is, right next to the seam, or ¼ inch away from the seam. In-the-ditch quilting needs no marking. For ¼-inch outline quilting, you can work by eye or use ¼-inch-wide masking tape as a guide for stitching. These and other straight lines can also be marked ligltly with a pencil and ruler.

Another type of quilting that needs no marking is called echo quilting. Look at the photo of August (page 40) for a beautiful example of this type of quilting. It contains lines of quilting that outline the sunflowers in concentric rings or shapes. The lines are generally spaced about ½ inch apart.

In contrast to outline and echo quilting, which need no marking, quilting designs should be marked before the quilt top is layered with batting and backing. How you mark depends on whether your fabric is light or dark.

Marking Light Fabrics

If your fabric is a light color that you can see through, such as muslin, you can place the pattern under the quilt top and easily trace the quilting design onto the fabric. First, either trace the design out of the book onto good-quality tracing paper or photocopy it. If necessary, darken the lines with a black permanent marker. If the pattern will be used many times, glue it to cardboard to make it sturdy. Place the pattern under the quilt top and carefully mark the designs on the fabric, making a thin, continuous line that will be covered by the quilting thread. Use a silver quilter's pencil or a mechanical pencil with thin (0.5 mm) medium (B) lead.

Marking Dark Fabrics

Use a white or silver pencil to mark quilting designs on dark fabrics. Mark from the top by drawing around a hard-edged quilting design template. To make simple templates, trace the design onto template plastic and cut out around the outer edge. Then trace around the outer edge of the template onto the fabric, and add inner lines by eye.

You may be able to use the method described above (placing the pattern underneath the fabric) if you place the pattern and the fabric on a light box while marking. The light shining through the paper and fabric will allow you to see the pattern outline through even the darkest fabrics. Any glass-topped table makes an excellent light box area. Simply take the lamp shade off of a small lamp, then place the lamp under the table. Tape your pattern to the tabletop, place the fabric on top of the pattern, and trace the pattern onto the fabric.

Quilt Backings

For each of the projects in this book, the list of fabrics and supplies includes yardage for the quilt back. For wallhangings that are narrower than 44 inches, simply use a full width of yardage cut several inches longer than the quilt top. For the wider wallhangings and most of the bed quilts, the quilt backing must be pieced unless you purchase extra-wide fabric, such as 90- or 108-inch-wide muslin.

Whenever possible, piece quilt backings in two or three panels with the seams running parallel to the long side of the quilt. Backs for quilts narrower than 80 inches wide can easily be pieced this way out of two lengths of yardage. Divide the yardage in half crosswise. Then, to avoid having a seam down the center of the quilt back, divide one of the pieces in half lengthwise. Sew a narrow panel to each side of a full-width central panel, as shown in **Diagram 25.** Be sure to trim the selvages from the yardage before joining the panels. Press the seams away from the center of the quilt.

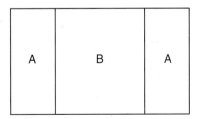

Diagram 25: Divide the yardage in half crosswise; divide one of the pieces in half lengthwise. Sew one of those halves to each side of the full-width piece, as shown.

For some quilts, you may make more sensible use of your yardage by piecing the back so that the seams run parallel to the short side of the quilt, as shown in **Diagram 26.** Some large quilts require 10 or more yards of backing fabric. To have the seams run parallel to the long side of the quilt, you would need three 3⅓-yard-long panels, for a total of 10 yards of fabric. However, if the seams run parallel to the shorter sides of a quilt, you would probably need three panels, each approximately 2¾ yards long, for a total of 8¼ yards of fabric, saving at least one yard of fabric.

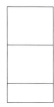

Diagram 26: Divide the yardage crosswise into three equal panels. Sew the three full-width panels together side by side; the seams should run parallel to the short side of the quilt top. Trim the excess from one panel as needed.

To prepare the backing, divide the yardage crosswise into three panels. Trim the selvages and sew the full-width panels together along their long sides; see **Diagram 26.**

Layering and Basting

Follow the procedure here for successful layering. If you plan to quilt by hand, baste with thread. If you will be machine quilting, use safety pins. Thread basting does not hold the layers securely enough during the machine quilting process. The thread is also more difficult to remove when quilting is completed.

For best results when thread basting large quilts, work at two or three banquet-type tables at a community center, library, or church basement. For pin basting, the best area is a large, clear area on the living room floor with carpet you can pin through when spreading out the quilt back.

Layering

1. Fold the quilt back in half lengthwise and press to form a centerline. Place the back, wrong side up, on the basting table. Position the pressed centerline at the middle of the table. To keep the backing taut, use pieces of masking tape at the corners or clamp it to the table with large binder clips from a stationery store.

2. Fold the batting in half lengthwise and lay it on the quilt backing, aligning the fold with the pressed centerline. Open out the batting; smooth and pat down any wrinkles.

3. Fold the quilt top in half lengthwise, right sides together, and lay it on the batting, aligning the fold with the center of the batting. Unfold the top; smooth it out and remove any loose threads. Make sure the backing and batting are at least 2 inches larger than the quilt top on all four sides for smaller projects. For bed-size quilts, add 3 inches extra on each side.

Basting

For hand quilting, use a long darning needle and white sewing thread to baste the layers together, making lines of basting approximately 4 inches apart. Baste from the center out in a radiating pattern, or make horizontal and vertical lines of

basting in a lattice fashion, using the seams that join the blocks as guidelines.

For machine quilting, use 1-inch safety pins to secure the layers together, pinning from the center out approximately every 3 inches. Do not place the pins where you intend to quilt. You may need as many as 1,000 pins to pin baste a queen-size quilt.

Quilting

Many of the projects in this book are hand quilted, but a few are machine quilted. Whether you will be stitching by hand or by machine, the tips that follow can help with your quilting.

Hand Quilting

- Use a hoop or frame to hold the quilt layers taut and smooth during quilting.

- Use short quilting needles, called betweens, in either size 9 or 10.

- Use quilting thread rather than regular sewing thread. Start with a length of quilting thread about 18 inches long. This is long enough to keep you going for a while, but not so long that it tangles easily.

- Pop the knot through the fabric at the beginning and end of each length of thread so that no knots show on the quilt front or back. To do this, insert the needle through the top and batting about 1 inch away from where you will begin stitching. Bring the needle to the surface in position to make the first stitch. Gently tug on the thread to pop the knot through the top and bury it in the batting, as shown in **Diagram 27.**

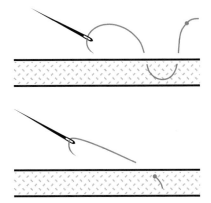

Diagram 27: Insert the needle through the top and batting, and gently tug on the thread until the knot pops through the fabric.

- Quilt by making running stitches, about $\frac{1}{16}$ to $\frac{1}{8}$ inch long, through all three layers. Try to keep the stitches straight and even.
- Thread several needles with quilting thread before you begin, and keep them handy while you work. This way you won't have to stop and thread a needle every time you finish a length of thread.

Machine Quilting

- Use a walking foot (also called an even feed foot) on your sewing machine for quilting straight lines. Use a darning or machine embroidery foot for free-motion quilting.
- To secure the thread at the beginning and end of a design, take several short stitches.
- *For free-motion quilting:* Disengage the sewing machine feed dogs so you can manipulate and move the quilt freely as you quilt. (Check your sewing machine manual to see how to do this.)
- Choose continuous-line quilting designs so you won't

have to begin and end threads as frequently as with interrupted designs. There will also be fewer threads to cut after you've finished quilting.

- Guide the marked design under the needle with both hands, working at an even pace so stitches will be of a consistent length.

Making and Attaching Binding

Double-fold binding is recommended for bed quilts. The bias or straight-grain binding strip is folded in half, and the raw edges are stitched to the edge of the quilt on the right side. The folded edge is then brought to the back of the quilt, as shown in **Diagram 28,** and hand stitched

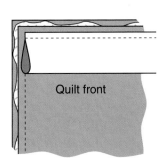

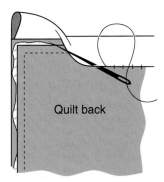

Diagram 28: For double-fold binding, fold the strip in half and stitch it to the quilt front. Bring the folded edge to the back of the quilt and hand stitch it in place.

in place. double-fold binding is easier to apply than single-fold binding, and its double thickness adds durability. The strips for this type of binding are cut four times the finished width plus seam allowances. As a general rule, cut the strips 2 inches wide for quilts with thin batting such as cotton and $2\frac{1}{4}$ inches wide for quilts with thicker batting. Most of the project directions in this book specify double-fold binding, and the fabric yardages are based on that type of binding.

If you wish to make single-fold binding, cut your fabric strips twice the width of your finished binding plus $\frac{1}{2}$ inch for seam allowances. Press under $\frac{1}{4}$ inch on one long edge of the binding. This edge will be hand sewn to the back of the quilt. Stitch the other long edge of the binding to the quilt top, right sides together. Fold the binding to the quilt back and stitch in place.

The amount of binding needed for each project is included with the finishing instructions. Generally, you will need the perimeter of the quilt plus 10 to 12 inches for mitering corners and ending the binding. Three-quarters to 1 yard of fabric will usually make enough binding to finish a large quilt.

Follow the instructions here to make continuous-cut bias binding or to join straight strips for continuous straight-grain binding. Unless the project directions tell you otherwise, sew the binding to the quilt as described below, mitering the binding at the corners.

Continuous-Cut Bias Binding

Continuous-cut bias binding is cut in one long strip from a

square of fabric that has been cut apart and resewn into a tube. You must first determine the size of the square you will need. To make approximately 400 inches of 2- or 2¼-inch-wide double-fold binding, enough to bind most bed quilts, start with a 30-inch square. If you don't have enough fabric for one large square, use several smaller squares. To estimate the number of inches of binding a particular square will produce, use this formula:

Multiply the length of one side by the length of another side. Divide the result by the width of binding you want.

Using a 30-inch square and 2¼-inch binding as an example: 30 × 30 = 900; 900 ÷ 2¼ = 400 inches of binding.

Seven Steps to Continuous-Cut Binding

1. Once you have determined the size you need, measure and cut a square of fabric.

2. Fold the square in half diagonally and press lightly. Cut the square into two triangles, cutting on the fold line.

3. Place the two triangles, right sides together, as shown in **Diagram 29.** Sew the pieces together, taking a ¼-inch seam. Open out the two pieces and press the seam open. The re-

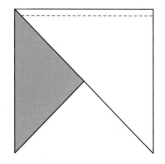

Diagram 29: Place the triangles right sides together as shown and stitch.

sulting piece should look like the one shown in **Diagram 30.**

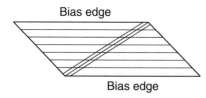

Bias edge

Bias edge

Diagram 30: Open out the two pieces and press the seam open. On the wrong side, mark cutting lines parallel to the bias edges.

4. Referring to **Diagram 30,** mark cutting lines on the wrong side of the fabric in the desired binding width. Mark parallel to the bias edges.

5. Fold the fabric right sides together, bringing the two non-bias edges together and offsetting them by one strip width, as shown in **Diagram 31.** Pin the edges together, creating a tube, and sew, taking a ¼-inch seam. Press the seam open.

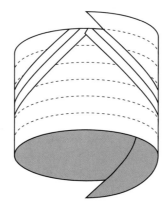

Diagram 31: Bring the nonbias edges together, offsetting them by one strip width. Sew the edges together to create a tube.

6. Cut on the marked lines, as shown in **Diagram 32,** turning the tube as you cut one long bias strip.

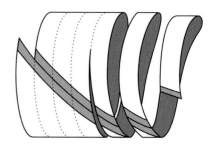

Diagram 32: Turning the tube as you go, cut along the marked lines to make one long bias strip.

7. To make double-fold binding, fold the long strip in half lengthwise, wrong sides together, and press.

Straight-Grain Binding

Straight-grain binding is easier to prepare than bias binding. Simply cut strips on the crosswise grain of the fabric and sew them together end to end with diagonal seams to get the required length. Although it isn't as flexible as bias binding, it is fine for straight-edge quilts.

Simple Straight-Grain Binding Method

1. Refer to the project instructions for the amount of binding the quilt requires. Estimate and cut the needed number of strips. When possible, cut the straight strips across the width of the fabric rather than along the length so they are slightly stretchy and easier to use.

2. Join the strips, as shown in **Diagram 33.** Place them right sides together, with each strip set in ¼ inch from the end of the other strip. Sew a diagonal seam. Trim the excess, leaving a ¼-inch seam. Continue adding strips until you have the length needed. For double-fold binding, fold and press the long strip in half lengthwise, with wrong sides together.

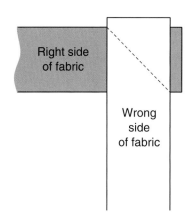

Diagram 33: Place the strips right sides together, positioning each strip ¼ inch in from the end of the other strip. Join with a diagonal seam.

Preparing a Quilt for Binding

Wait to trim excess batting and backing until after the binding is stitched to the top of the quilt. If the edges of the quilt are uneven after quilting, use a ruler and pencil to mark a placement line for the binding, as close as possible to the raw edges of the quilt top. This will give you a guideline against which you can align the raw edge of the binding strip. For best results, use a ruled square to mark the placement lines at the corners.

If you have a walking or even feed foot for your sewing machine, use it in place of the regular presser foot when sewing on the binding. If you do not have a walking foot, thread baste around the quilt along the edges to hold the layers firmly together during binding and to avoid puckers.

Attaching the Binding

1. Once you have made your binding strips (using either the continuous-cut bias or straight-

grain strip method), you must prepare them so they can be attached to the quilt. If you are using double-fold binding, fold the long strip in half lengthwise, wrong sides together, and press. If you are using single-fold binding, you must fold over ¼ inch along one long side of the strip and press.

2. Begin attaching the binding in the middle of a side, not in a corner. Place the binding strip right sides together with the quilt top, with the raw edges of the binding strip even with the raw edge of the quilt top (or the drawn placement line).

3. Fold over the beginning raw edge of the binding approximately 1 inch, as shown in **Diagram 34.** Securing the stitches with a backstitch, begin sewing ½ inch from the fold. Sew the binding to the quilt, stitching through all layers, ¼ inch from the raw edge of the binding.

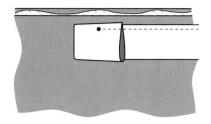

Diagram 34: Fold the raw edge back about 1 inch, and begin stitching ½ inch from the fold. Backstitch to anchor the stitching.

4. When you are approaching a corner, stop stitching exactly ¼ inch away from the raw edge of the corner. Backstitch and remove the quilt from the sewing machine, clipping threads.

5. Fold the binding up and away from the corner, as shown in **Diagram 35A,** forming a 45 degree angle fold.

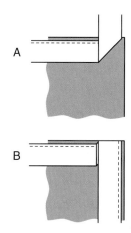

Diagram 35: Stop stitching ¼ inch from the corner and fold the binding up at a 45 degree angle (A). Fold the binding strip back down, align the raw edges with the side of the quilt top, and stitch the binding in place (B).

6. Fold the binding strip back down and align the raw edges with the adjacent side of the corner, as shown in **Diagram 35B.**

7. Begin stitching the next side at the top raw edge of the quilt, as shown in **Diagram 35B.** The fold created in the fabric is essential; it provides the fullness necessary to fit around the corners as you fold the binding to the back side of the quilt. Miter all four corners in this manner.

8. As you approach the point where you began, cross the folded-back beginning section with the ending section. Sew across the fold, as shown in **Diagram 36;** allow the end section

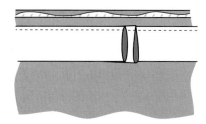

Diagram 36: Cross the beginning section with the ending section, overlapping them about ½ inch.

to extend approximately ½ inch beyond the binding.

9. Trim away the excess batting and backing, using scissors or a rotary cutter and a ruler. Before you trim the whole quilt, fold over a small section and turn the binding to the back of the quilt to determine the right amount of excess to trim. The binding will look best and wear longer if it is filled rather than hollow.

10. Turn the binding to the back of the quilt and blindstitch the folded edge in place, covering the machine stitches with the folded edge. Finish the miters at the corners by folding in the adjacent sides on the back of the quilt and placing several stitches in the miter, as shown in **Diagram 37.** Add several stitches to the miters on the front in the same manner.

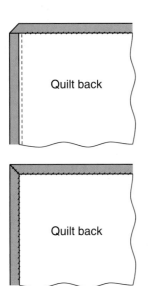

Diagram 37: Blindstitch the binding in place on the quilt back. Fold in the adjacent corner and stitch along the miter.

If you plan to add a hanging sleeve, follow the directions below to make and attach the sleeve before turning and finishing the binding.

Adding a Hanging Sleeve

If you plan to display your quilt, at home or at a quilt show, you will certainly need to add a hanging sleeve to the back.

The best way to prepare any of the wallhangings in this book for display is to add a hanging sleeve when you are binding the quilt. A rod or dowel can be inserted in the sleeve and supported by nails or hooks on the wall. Many quilters put hanging sleeves on bed quilts as well so that their work can be exhibited at quilt shows. Use the following procedure to add a 4-inch-wide hanging sleeve, which can accommodate a 2-inch-diameter dowel or pole.

1. Cut a strip of muslin or other fabric that is 8½ inches wide and 1 inch shorter than the width of the finished quilt.

2. Machine hem the short ends. To hem, turn under ½ inch on each end of the strip and press. Turn under another ½ inch and stitch next to the pressed fold.

3. Fold and press the strip in half lengthwise, wrong sides together, aligning the two long raw edges.

4. Position the raw edges of the sleeve to align with the top raw edges on the back of the quilt, centering the sleeve on the quilt. The binding should already

be sewn on the front, but not turned to the back of the quilt. Pin the sleeve in place.

5. Machine stitch the sleeve to the back of the quilt, stitching from the front by sewing on top of the stitches that hold the binding to the quilt.

6. Turn the binding to the back of the quilt and hand stitch it in place so that the binding covers the raw edge of the sleeve, as shown in **Diagram 38.** When turning the binding on the edge that has the sleeve, you may need to trim away more batting and backing in order to turn the binding easily.

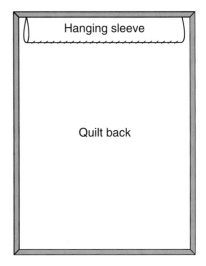

Diagram 38: Stitch the raw edge of the sleeve to the top of the quilt. Bring the binding to the back of the quilt and hand stitch it in place, covering the top raw edge of the sleeve. Then, hand stitch the bottom edge of the sleeve to the quilt back.

7. Hand stitch the bottom loose edge of the sleeve in place, being careful not to sew through to the front of the quilt.

Acknowledgments

Konnichiwa by Suzanne Marshall, Clayton, Missouri. Inspired by the World's Fair block in *The Quilter's Album of Blocks and Borders* by Jinny Beyer, Suzanne added Japanese cotton *yukata* (summer kimono) fabrics, original borders, and unique quilting designs to create a scrap quilt with a geometric feel. Konnichiwa has appeared in many quilt shows, some of which include the 1993 Rockome Gardens Quilt Celebration in Arcola, Illinois, where it was awarded best of show. It was also shown at the 1993 AIQA Quilt Festival in Houston, Texas, where it placed third in the Traditional Pieced Division. Suzanne was selected to be included in the "30 Distinguished Quilt Artists of the World Exhibit" in Tokyo, Japan, during 2003.

Overwhelmed by Autumn by Diane Doro, Des Moines, Iowa. Diane made her first quilt in 1980 while awaiting the birth of her first child. She used cardboard templates and scissors to cut the pieces, and she says it might have been her last quilt if her mother-in-law (a non-quilter) hadn't helped her finish the cutting. Diane is a member of the Des Moines Area Quilter's Guild and has helped with fund-raising and service projects and has assisted the guild's librarian.

Yellow Monday by Elsie Moser, Dorchester, Ontario, Canada. Elsie loves designing quilts. For Yellow Monday, she made 91 blocks and, of those, selected just 64 for the final quilt. She's been a quilter for almost 20 years and is a member of the Ingersol Creative Art Centre and Oxford's Quilter's Guild. Yellow Monday was exhibited at the 1994 American Quilter's Society show, where it won best wall quilt in the Amateur Division. It also received the judges' choice award at the Canadian Quilter's Association in Halifax, Nova Scotia.

Basket Pillowcases by Sandra Barford, Doylestown, Pennsylvania. Sandra designed these miniature basket pillowcases to match her bed quilt, as well as to exhibit them in the 1994 Variable Star Quilters quilt show in Harleysville, Pennsylvania. She especially enjoyed them because they gave her a chance to work in pastels. She has been a quilter since 1979 and enjoys designing, making, and collecting quilts.

Thanksgiving Wall Quilt by Kathy Berschneider, Rockford, Illinois. Kathy works as a secretary and administrative assistant at an elementary school and finds sewing and quilting relaxing at the end of a workday. She has also taught classes, clerked, and made display items for a local quilt shop. She loves designing her own projects and created this original wall hanging using a block called Indian Trails from *1001 Patchwork Designs* by Maggie Malone.

Scrap Baskets by Kris Merkens, Ada, Minnesota. Kris prefers hand piecing and hand quilting traditional designs. The pattern she used for this quilt was by Susan Bartlett of The Quilted Cottage in Erie, Pennsylvania. Scrap Baskets was exhibited at the 1991 Indian Summer Quilt Show in Fargo, North Dakota, where it was awarded First Place in the Small Quilts category.

August by Norma Grasse, Silverdale, Pennsylvania. Norma made August for the 1992 Variable Star Quilters' show, where it received first prize. She has been quilting since 1978 and particularly likes traditional quilts. Appliqué designs are especially appealing to her, because she finds them relaxing to stitch. August was shown in the 1994 American Quilter's Society show in Paducah, Kentucky, and it appeared in the 1995 AQS Quilt Art Calendar.

Jim's Scrappy Nine Patch by Gloria Greenlee, Cheyenne, Wyoming. Gloria likes traditional quilts best, as this scrap quilt demonstrates. And although she enjoys the hand quilting process, she also does a lot of machine quilting in order to complete more quilts. This quilt was exhibited at the Green Country Quilter's guild show in 1991; A Celebration of Quilts in Oklahoma City in 1991, where it was awarded Third Place in the Traditional Pieced Category; the Tulsa State Fair in 1990, where it was awarded First Place in the Machine Pieced/ Machine Quilted category; and Quilt America: 1991. Gloria began quilting in 1984 and has been designing and teaching since 1991.

Old Schoolhouse by Norma Grasse, Silverdale, Pennsylvania. Norma, a charter member of the Variable Star Quilters, collects old fabrics. She put her antique black and red fabrics to good use in this adaptation of the traditional schoolhouse quilt. Norma also used an antique template for the star flowers (or pinwheels) in the border. Old Schoolhouse was displayed at the 1993 Quilters' Heritage Celebration in Lancaster, Pennsylvania.

Brick Wall by Tina M. Gravatt, Philadelphia, Pennsylvania. Tina is a teacher, lecturer, and author whose historically accurate miniatures have appeared in many exhibitions and publications. This miniature is a reproduction of the full-size antique, which she found in an antique shop in upstate New York. The miniature was exhibited at the Museum of the American Quilter's Society in 1992 and was featured at the Quilters' Heritage Celebration in 1992 as part of an invited special exhibit entitled "Reconstructing the Past."

Patchwork Pillows by Cyndi Hershey, Audubon, Pennsylvania. Cyndi was inspired to start quilting in 1976 by the Great American Quilt Contest sponsored by *Good Housekeeping* magazine. With an education in interior design and textiles, quilting was a natural fit! Cyndi and her husband purchased The Country Quilt Shop in Montgomeryville, Pennsylvania, in 1989. The shop was selected as one of the Top Ten Quilt Shops in 1999 by *American Patchwork and Quilting* magazine. Cyndi and her husband owned the shop for more than 10 years. She currently works as Merchandise Consultant for P&B Textiles and is involved with product development and their design department. Cyndi enjoys freelance editing for several quilt book publishers.

Country Wedding Ring by Susan Stein, White Bear Township, Minnesota. The traditional Double Wedding Ring is one of Susan's favorite quilt patterns. She has made 58 of them—even one with 100 rings! She likes to combine unusual fabrics and give her quilts unique textural treatments to create special effects. Sometimes she cuts fabrics slightly off-grain for a whimsical, folk art look. She has been a quilter for 26 years and in that time has made more than 400 quilts ranging from wallhangings to bed size. Susan owns a store called Colorful Quilts and Textiles in St. Paul, which features unusual fabrics from around the world, contemporary commercial fabrics, and the work of 10 hand-dyers. She is the author of *Double Wedding Ring Quilts: Coming Full Circle*, published by AQS.

Plaid Folk Hearts by Roberta Horton, Berkeley, California. Roberta has been a quiltmaker for more than 30 years. During her career she has authored six quiltmaking books. She teaches and lectures internationally. Believing that fabric is the inspiration for her quilts, she is intent on learning to listen to what it has to say, and then following those dictates.

Stargazing with Roberta and **Stargazing with Roberta Miniature** by Karen Hull Sienk, Colden, New York. Karen made these quilts using many of Roberta Horton's plaid fabrics. Her employer liked the large version so much, he asked if he could purchase it from her. Not wanting to part with her quilt, Karen decided to make a miniature version of the large quilt for him. It turned out nicely, so she made another to be able to keep one for herself. She is an active member of the Southtowns Piecemakers group. Stargazing with Roberta appeared in the 1994 Quilters' Heritage Celebration in Lancaster, Pennsylvania. Karen teaches workshops, and she lectures for guilds and local quilt shops.

Escargot in Plaid by Shelby Morris, Cartersville, Georgia. Shelby feels that she has always been a quiltmaker at heart, but she didn't actually make her first quilt until 1977. She belongs to the Etowah Valley Quilter's Guild in Cartersville, Georgia, which grew out of a beginner's class she taught there in 1991. Shelby also belongs to the East Cobb Quilters Guild and the American Quilter's Society. Escargot in Plaid has been shown at the 1993 Georgia Celebrates Quilts show, by the East Cobb Quilter's Guild, and at the 1994 American Quilter's Society show in Paducah, Kentucky. Shelby has made about 130 quilts ranging in size from miniature to king, but she says if she could keep only one quilt, it would be "Escargot in Plaid."

Plaid Spools by Kim Baird, Fargo, North Dakota. Kim has been quilting since 1978. Her favorite quilts are strong, graphic designs; she likes antique scrap quilts as well as contemporary art pieces. Kim lets her quilts "evolve," starting with a pattern and some color ideas and just making blocks until there are enough. From 1983 to 1985, Kim headed the North Dakota Quilt Project, which documented more than 3,500 quilts. Plaid Spools was exhibited at the 1991 Indian Summer Quilt Show in Fargo, North Dakota, and appeared in the 1991 American Quilter's Society "Quilt Art Engagement Calendar."

Baskets of Love by Connie Rodman, West Fargo, North Dakota. Connie joined the Quilters' Guild of North Dakota in 1986 at the urging of her aunt. She thought she'd have nothing in common with a bunch of quilters but soon found that she fit right in. In fact, it was her guild that pieced the baskets in this quilt. Baskets of Love won

both the Guild Award and the Teacher's Award at her guild's 1991 Indian Summer Quilt Show. Connie won Best of Show at the Indian Summer Quilt Show for two other quilts in 2001 and 2002. Connie is a member of a small appliqué group, which shares projects and techniques. She teaches quilting classes at her local fabric store.

Pineapple Askew by Nancy Ota, San Clemente, California. Nancy says quilting became her passion after taking quilting classes offered at the Adult Education Center in San Juan Capistrano in 1988. She actively participates in two quilt guilds and was the president of the Beach Cities Quilters Guild from 1994 to 1995. She works as a dental hygienist, teaches quilting, gives trunk shows to share her work, and creates and sells patterns for quilters. Pineapple Askew was a finalist in the 1993 Pacific International Quilt Show, the 1994 American Quilter's Society show, and won a blue ribbon at the 1994 Orange County Fair.

Twist and Shout by Sue Nickels, Ann Arbor, Michigan. Sue's inspiration for Twist and Shout came from attending a Beaver Island retreat with Gwen Marston, where she enjoyed learning freeform piecing. A quilter for more than 25 years, Sue focuses on machine techniques in teaching her classes and giving lectures. Twist and Shout was exhibited at the 1994 American Quilter's Society show in Paducah, Kentucky. Sue's quilt "The Beatle Quilt," made with her sister Pat Holly, won the AQS Best of Show award in 1998.

Gemstones by Jeanne Jenzano, Aldan, Pennsylvania. Jeanne is a member of Undercover Quilters in Aston, Delaware County, Pennsylvania. She loves scrap quilts because she is always amazed that so many different fabrics can work so well together. Jeanne pieced Gemstones in jewel-toned scraps for a wedding gift for her son and daughter-in-law. Gemstones won third place in the Undercover Quilt Show in 1993 and was also selected as a juried quilt in the 1993 Quilters' Heritage Celebration.

Tessellating Sea Horses by Donna Radner, Chevy Chase, Maryland. Donna has been a quiltmaker since 1981. Coordinated scrap quilts are her favorites because she likes to use as many fabrics as possible in her quilts. Tessellating Sea Horses was shown at the 1993 Quilters' Heritage Celebration in Lancaster, Pennsylvania, and at the 1993 American Quilter's Society show in Paducah, Kentucky. Donna's more recent work has become more free-form, with irregular-shaped pieces and curvy pieced strips. Batiks and brighter colors predominate in her newer quilts. She is currently teaching classes that show quilters how to make fabric strips into fractured Log Cabin and tilted square designs.

Princess Feather and Rose of Sharon by Dana Klein, Dallas, Texas. Her inspiration came from a photo of an antique quilt in *Quilt Digest 3*. Dana's interpretation has won several awards, including Second Place/Appliqué at the Dallas Quilt Guild Show in 1989; Second Place/Appliqué/Artisan at the Houston Quilt Festival in 1989; and Second Place/Appliqué and Judges' Choice at the Quilters' Heritage Celebration in 1990.